Becoming Whole:

For Such A time As this

A guided journey to freedom and inner healing

Becoming Whole:
For Such A Time As This

A guided journey to freedom and inner healing.

Written by:

Rochelle Frazier Foster

Chase Bridges Press

Becoming Whole: For Such A Time As This
First Edition ©2017 by Rochelle Frazier Foster

Cover Design By: Zizi Iryaspraha S
www.pagatana.com
Edited By: Heidi Vine

All stories in this book have changed names of people in effort
to protect their privacy.

ISBN 978-1-64008-952-5

Printed in the United States of America

First Printing May 2017/Printed in the United States of America

A.W. Tozer said, "The reason why many are still troubled, still seeking, still making little forward progress is because they haven't yet come to the end of themselves. We're still trying to give orders, and interfering with God's work within us." Perhaps we have arrived at the moment of coming to our end, releasing our identity as victim and our need to blame, and instead tending to the garden of our soul in effort to find what is fully available…

freedom,

intimacy, and

destiny!

CONTENTS

INTRODUCTION

Lost in an American Gospel that left not even a remnant of Jesus, I realized that my life was full, but my soul was empty. Because I was raised in church, I never looked up to be filled, even though the hunger grew uncontrollably. Instead I looked to my career, my home, my handbag, and my social status to fill something I couldn't name, but these things only intensified the hunger. Still, believing I had it all together, I prayed for the 'lost,' assuming they were the poor, broken, and marginalized, only to discover that I was comfortably sitting in the walls of what today we call 'church,' and I was *still* lost. I had the 'God card' checked in every way, meeting every requirement the church looked for to validate me worthy and righteous, yet I missed Him completely. Eventually I had to learn that the building was never meant to be the church: I was —and you are— too!

A piece of my awakening came when I ventured past the self absorbed portion of Jeremiah 29:11 that I had so often clung to—*For I know the plans I have for you, declares The Lord*—and found the rest of the story—*And when you seek with all of your heart, I will be found and I will bring you back from captivity.* I was a captive who was DANGEROUSLY DECEIVED that I was living out the full "christian" experience. You see, I was the woman that many would have believed knew God intimately, and the truth was that I didn't know Him *at all.* I knew the Word. I knew the commands, but I had never met the Author. Knowing the depth of my own deception, I have to believe that the modern day churches are full of captives too.

Julian of Norwich said, "First there is the fall, and then the recovery from the fall. But *both* are the mercy of God." Her words are my experience. It was when my perfectly designed life finally broke into a million little pieces that I began, out of desperation, to look up. It was at this point when I learned that sometimes it takes feeling alone and deep down in the pit to truly find HIM. After 31 years in church, I began to grasp that 'Beloved' is not a word you read or claim, but it is something you know deep in your soul to be your reality! And when you know it, a 7th grade crush gone bad, or an absent father, or a broken marriage can't take from you the truth that you are dearly, deeply, and fiercely loved by God. We are drawn to love and we long to be loved, not because we are weak or needy, but rather because we are divinely woven to be restless without it.

I believe we are on the verge of a great revival of love, and I sense that He is using women to release this movement of love. The hearts of women will be made whole again. A holy passion for His presence will be imparted. And the voices of the masses sharing the love of a good, good Father will be unleashed to heal nations!

Like most women I am drawn to the story of Esther, I believe Esther's story is *our* story. I believe God showed us the desire of His heart through her life to move us from an orphan spirit to that of an heir to His Kingdom. I believe when we realize who we are in Christ, we begin to walk as Esther did: in favor, influence, boldness, and identity. Only then —from true identity— can we live out our divine DESTINY!

I believe we are living in a "For Such A Time As This" season, where modern day Esthers are being RELEASED. These women will walk in divine favor, shifting atmospheres in their homes, communities, and even nations. They will be wrapped in an infectious love of the Father. No longer held captive by fear, or depression, or self-doubt, "Fiercely loved" will be their new identity. They will understand the balance between soaking in His love and slaying demons in His name, and make time for both! They will have voices of influence and authority, and begin reclaiming territory for the Kingdom. They will carry a boldness through the empowering of the Holy Spirit that will cause others to rise with them. They will know who their real enemy is and freely release all they have held captive to the pain of their hearts.

The Holy Spirit led me to study this 'soaking' season that was part of Esther's protocol to the inner courts of the palace. For six months, these women would have beauty treatments including being soaked in Myrrh, a purifying agent. To be worthy of the presence of the King, they would have to purify themselves from the tainting of the world. After this six month 'detox season,' they would then spend the next six months being fragranced so that they released a heavenly aroma.

So I'm lead to ponder: What aroma are we leaving? Is it a sweet aroma of grace and mercy? Is it an aroma of love and gentleness? Peace and joy? Or perhaps it is a bitter or calloused scent? Or could it be one that is cold and controlling? Unforgiving and judgmental?

There is no doubt that our lives leak. Our hope should be that what we are leaking is an aroma that draws people closer to the heart of the Father. If we truly desire to be that scent of heaven, then we must deal with or 'soak off' the bitter roots that hinder the flow of love God intended.

I have found that many of us, with good intentions, try to live out our destiny while burying our past wounds and failures. We believe we can let the past be the past, and we have missed the damaging impact it has had on our relationships, the interference with intimacy it has caused between us and the Father, and the roadblocks it has placed around living out our destiny. It is not enough to bury our past. We must lay an axe to the roots of our problems, uproot them, and replace the gaping holes in our hearts with the love of the Father. His love, rooted deep within, will compel us to live from destiny without striving or performing, but rather from a place of acceptance and love. Finally realizing who we are in Christ, and how fiercely He loves us, will propel us into destiny. A destiny He *longs* for us to fulfill!

In this journal, we will soak in the Holy Spirit as Esther did in Myrrh, surrendering our souls to the purifying power of His indwelling Spirit. Ultimately, we are bringing our broken hearts to the table of the Great Physician, inviting Him to shine His perfect light into the depths of our root system, exposing all that hinders the intimacy, identity, and destiny He planned for us. We will look at some toxic theology that keeps us comfortably out of the Kingdom of God. We will tend to the wounded soul, remove the enemy's assignments on our lives from our words, vows, and judgements, and identify patterns that steal our inheritance. We focus on freedom and healing, because a wounded soul can hinder intimacy with the Father and block your divine assignments that are birthed from intimacy.

Divine assignments are given in the secret place—the place you are most fully connected to the heart of the Father. As you "soak," you will remove barriers to that sacred place, so that you can connect intimately and live out passionately *His* assignment on your life. I suggest you take this process as slow as you need to in order to do the work. Denial and "stuffing" our emotions will not lead to restoration and can no longer be our default. Sometimes we must go back to our pain just one more time to allow God to heal it. But press on: The good news is that He longs to redeem you[1] and He promises to never leave you or forsake you.[2] He is just *waiting* for you to grab a hold of His hand, and allow Him to lead you into deeper waters. Beloved, you *WERE* made **FOR SUCH A TIME AS THIS!**

SECTION ONE:

The
Foundation

CHAPTER ONE:

AN INVITATION TO SOAK

My soul is restless until if finds rest in thee.
Saint Augustine

Our culture keeps us busy and even honors us for our plates that are over flowing, seeking to keep up with the demands of hyper-driven schedules. It seems to be the marking of a good mother to be *so* busy! Perhaps there is great wisdom in the words of your airline flight attendant: "In the event that the cabin pressure should drop, please put on your own mask before assisting others." It seems so noble to sacrifice for the sake of those around you, yet the souls of women are eroding due to exhaustion from trying to keep up, or perhaps live up, to the cultural expectations of the modern day woman.

I feel compelled to say that the air pressure has dropped, and it is time to grab the oxygen mask and breathe. Yes, you have permission to rest. It is actually the most spiritual thing you can do in this season. There is a reason that He calls us to be still, because it is only in stillness that we know Him, and only in stillness that we find an identity that will break off the striving that drives us to the chaotic schedules in the first place.

I have been one to mark spiritual change by a physical activation or marking. This idea of physical activation or marking is seen throughout the Word of God: Jacob encounters God and receives a name change {Israel}, he then marks the spot with a stone pillar signifying it was the place he met with God.[3] After the Israelites crossed over the Jordan River on dry ground, Joshua instructed the people to place twelve stones representing the twelve tribes of Israel as a memorial for the people of God to remember how God had saved them.[4] When Elisha received the mantle of Elijah, he not only stepped into that new identity, but he burned the thing that marked his past, his plow.[5] Elisha would never be tempted to go back to the life God called him out of as an oxen driver, if he burned the very thing he needed to fulfill that role. I recall having a ceremony in my back yard burning items and pictures that held memories to pieces of my life that God called me out of. I suppose it declares over your life that you are *choosing* to shift or turn.

I love the words of 2 Corinthians 3: 16-17:

But whenever anyone turns to the Lord, the veil is taken away. Now the Lord is the Spirit, and where the Spirit of the Lord is, there is freedom.

This same Spirit is like myrrh to our souls, purifying us from the wounds of the world: the heartache, the disappointments, the failures, and all of the beliefs that don't align to the identity we long to grab hold of. This same Spirit begins to change us from glory to glory until we behold, like in a mirror, the image of God. This says to me that the change the Spirit does in us will manifest physically. We will look differently at the woman in the mirror, and perhaps we will embrace her in her fullness, and not only accept her, but love her as well! So we mark this journey of soaking, as we soak!

Unfortunately, we don't get six months to experience beauty treatments as Esther did, but we ask God to honor our intention as we soak our hearts in His love while living in reality. This 'soaking' phase is designed to go deep to expose the roots that drive our lives. I have learned that sometimes we must go back one more time to lay an ax to the root, and then we make space for His love to grow. As His love grows, we organically begin to step into our true identity of Beloved! Sweet friend, you are dearly loved and designed to spill that love out onto the world. I love how

Graham Cooke says that we are designed to be God's visual aide of His love on earth. I don't know if you can grasp that concept in this moment, but my prayer is that when you finish this journey you look different!

Your First Assignment Is To Soak:

Detox Bath:
1/4 Cup Epson Salt
1/4 Cup Baking Soda
Lavender Essential Oil {Myrrh Oil —optional}

As you're soaking, offer up a prayer surrendering your heart to Him for this season of healing and freedom. In Psalm 46:10, He says to *Be still and know Him*. The Hebrew word for *know* is yada. This word yada would suggest an intimate knowing. This *knowing* could even birth something like we read in Genesis where Adam *knew* Eve and they bore a son.[6] I wonder….

Do you *know* Him?

Has that knowing *birthed* something in you?

We will begin to step into a new revelation of this calling to be still and open our hearts to a new way of *knowing* God. Today, may you release the weight on your shoulders and the weariness of your feet as you find rest in Him. You have permission today to SOAK!

I declare today that I am a modern day Esther. I am willing to surrender to the process of soaking to allow Your Holy Spirit to tend to my wounded soul, to free me from what hinders my connection to You, and to awaken me to my divine destiny. I invite Your Holy Spirit into the depths of my heart, and I say, "Have Your Way!" I surrender my rights to direct my path going forward, therefore, on the days that I am weak and begin to wander from Your path, strengthen me[7] and draw me back into Your loving presence. Help me maintain focus as I seek to fix my eyes upon You, and surrender my life to Your Lordship. May Your kindness keep me in a place of repentance,[8] so that I may find truth without resistance or denial. May the blinders of the enemy of this age be removed this day so that I see with clarity the hope to which You have called me[9]. May the hardened or calloused places of my heart be restored to Your original design so that I don't miss the life You destined for me[10]. I ask for the gift of unshakable faith, and the revelation of the love of the Father that goes beyond my comprehension that according to Your Word are available[11,12]. I declare that I was created for such a time as this, and I choose to live out everything You had in mind when You created me[13]. You, Father, are my heart's desire, and I find delight in Your Presence[14].

He speaks to my heart...

How did it feel to rest? Why is it such a struggle to tend to your own heart? Did He speak to you? Is there something you need to release?

_____

_____

_____

_____

_____

_____

_____

_____

_____

_____

_____

_____

_____

CHAPTER TWO:

The Mission Statement of Jesus

He has sent me to bind up the brokenhearted, to proclaim freedom for the captives and release from darkness for the prisoners. Isaiah 61: 1

My journey to freedom began about five years ago when I felt called to stir women to live from their Divine DNA. It was my first season to really break out of the "South"as a Bible teacher touching the North, South, East, and West of the United States. As I was ministering to women from different cities, I realized that there was one thing every city had in common: women in the church shared the same lies as the women lost in the world. In each city, I would use a wall or a box for women to write a lie they believed about themselves either on the wall or to be placed in the box. I didn't fully understand the power of freedom ministry at this point, but I knew the Lord had put in my spirit to awaken women to the divine thread of their hearts to be His Beloved, and to do this I would need to uproot the lies keeping them in bondage outside of His truth.

The words written on these walls or tucked in the boxes were the same in every city despite the location or culture: not enough, unseen, unworthy, disqualified, and rejected. The women that were invited from transitional homes or outreach programs used the same words as the church ladies, and even some of the women serving in ministry. I began to wrestle with these thoughts: How is it that the lies and internal struggles plaguing the lost and marginalized were the same lies and struggles haunting believers? Shouldn't Christ followers be living lives full of the fruits of the spirit? Where was the love? What about the joy? The peace? How could the lives of believers be so similar to those living without Jesus?

As I sought God in prayer, I was led to Isaiah 61 where the prophet speaks of one coming that would be anointed to basically shift atmospheres. This "anointed one" would have the ability to turn ashes to beauty, despair to a garment of praise, and mourning to joy. He would release prisoners from darkness and free captives. He would make us a righteous oak on display to show off His splendor.

Then I was led to the life of Jesus and the words of Luke:

And He came to Nazareth, where He had been brought up; and as was His custom, He entered the synagogue on the Sabbath, and stood up to read. And the book of the prophet Isaiah was handed to Him. And He opened the book and found the place where it was written, "The spirit of the Lord is upon me, because He anointed me to preach the gospel to the poor. He has sent me to proclaim release to captives and recovery of sight to the blind, to set free those who are oppressed, to proclaim the year of the Lord's favor." And He closed the book, gave it back to the attendant and sat down; and the eyes of all in the synagogue were fixed on Him. And He began to say to them, "Today this Scripture has been fulfilled in your hearing."

The words, *Today, this scripture has been fulfilled in your hearing,* was much like Jesus declaring His public mission statement from Isaiah 61. He came to bring freedom. He came to restore God's people. He came to put a spirit of praise and joy upon our lives that would override our despair. We can see from His ministry that He lived out this mission of Isaiah 61 bringing dead things to life, restoring sight to the spiritually and physically blind, bringing joy to those with despair, and setting prisoners free. Then as He took His last breath, He spoke this word: "TETE-LESTI" or *it is finished.*[15] So what Jesus came to do was complete; it was finished! He tore the veil that separated us from God giving us full access to the Father, He paid in full for our sin, He connected us back to our source, and He offered a life free and abundant.

I came that you would have life in the full.
John 10:10

With this fresh realization of the power of the cross, I began to question: if He offered such freedom and paid such a great price then why are so many 'followers' still dragging chains? In effort to find the answer, I pursued freedom ministry. I devoured numerous books on freedom, healing, and prayer. I attended encounters, conferences, healing centers, and prayer ministries searching for the answer. What I learned from this journey, I share with you here. Freedom is available, and the Father longs to restore our souls. However, we, in our humanity and fallen human condition, open doors to the enemy of our souls from words spoken that become lies, vows, and judgements. We open doors through sin. We open doors through generational iniquity—sins of our fathers. We open doors as we erect idols that vie for the places in our hearts that were meant for Him alone. Because this process goes deep, requires commitment, and sometimes is painful, you must know your **WHY!**

Why pursue freedom ministry?
Freedom ministry will change our relationships, so that we can enjoy vibrant, healthy relationships without offense, guilt, shame, or control.

Freedom ministry will remove lies that steal our joy and peace, and allow us to connect with the Father with new clarity.

Freedom ministry will help us break patterns that have controlled our lives and have kept us from our inheritance.

Freedom ministry will remove barriers to intimacy with the Father.

Freedom ministry will help us remove assignments that hinder our destiny.

Freedom ministry will help us step into new authority realizing truth and dismantling the strategies of the enemy to keep us captive.

Why freedom ministry? Because you are worth it! And somewhere deep down there is probably a lie that has kept you, like me, so busy putting the oxygen mask on others that you come here desperate for something more! There are things in your life that may be so familiar to you that you have decided they will always be a part of your life, but I am here to tell you that you can be free! It is time for you to grab hold of what is already available through Jesus Christ! The price has been paid for your freedom, now He invites us to step into LIVING FREE!

The good news is that the power of the cross and the testimony of Jesus covers the death in our words, our sin, and our generational iniquity. However, we must go back and close these doors that have given the enemy access to our lives. In going back to the root, we invite the Holy Spirit to come in and replace these lies with God's truth.

There is a simple protocol that we will use here to dismantle the power of the enemy in our lives. We will call this process The Five Rs, because there are five steps to breaking assignments and reclaiming the territory of your soul, and they all begin with the letter R.

RECOGNIZE
The first step is to simply RECOGNIZE we have an area of bondage. This means we confess that we have come into agreement with a lie, made a vow, or cast judgement that violates the Word of God. It may also be recognizing impure motives

of our hearts, or recognizing where we have withheld forgiveness, or recognizing we have generational iniquity in our bloodline. The first key is to RECOGNIZE!

REPENT

To REPENT is to TURN from the lie, vow, judgement, sin, idol, or bitterness. REPENTING calls us to renew our minds to His truth and live from that truth.

RENOUNCE

We must break the assignments that have been placed on our lives, because we have opened the door to the enemy by coming into agreement with him over God's truth. Jesus gave us the authority to RENOUNCE the power of the enemy.

RECEIVE

This step is often overlooked, but is detrimental in maintaining freedom. We must replace lies with truth, so we need to RECEIVE that truth. We ask the Holy Spirit to show us the truth about the circumstances where the lie entered into our lives, and what His truth says about our circumstances and us. We RECEIVE truth here.

REPLACE

Finally, we replace the lie with the truth.

I always recommend sealing this process by listening to the Holy Spirit, because often He will speak more truth if we are willing to listen. Knowing the nature of our enemy, we need to be prepared that he will come seeking to reenter the door once opened, so we must be prepared with the truth to resist his lie. I simply model what Jesus did in the desert when Satan came to tempt Him, I respond with my truth…

It is written _____.

For example, if my lie was 'I am alone' and the enemy is trying to convince me once again that I am alone, then I would say aloud: *It is written that I am never alone, because God never leaves me or forsakes me.* This truth helps you resist the devil each time he tempts you to come into agreement with his lies. We may all know the words of James 4, but have we implemented this truth into our lives? We must SUBMIT to God's truth, and RESIST the enemy's schemes to allure us into taking his bait.

Submit to God, resist the devil and he will flee.
James 4:7

We will discuss lies, vows, judgements, generational iniquity, and many other areas the enemy has used to keep us in bondage, but for now I just want you to grasp the understanding that we *need* to pursue freedom ministry. **You need** to pursue freedom ministry. This means YOU, not your mother or father or husband. This is about you. Your family may all need freedom ministry, because we all do, but for this moment this journey is about you finding your freedom. 'Free people can free people,' so we believe that as you walk in freedom you will light the paths for others around you to pursue their own freedom.

He speaks to my heart...

What is your why? What has brought you here? What do you hope to release? What do you hope to gain?

_____
_____
_____
_____
_____
_____
_____
_____
_____
_____
_____
_____
_____
_____
_____
_____
_____
_____
_____
_____
_____
_____
_____
_____
_____
_____

CHAPTER THREE:

The Key To Freedom

But whenever a person turns to the Lord, the veil is taken away. Now the Lord is the Spirit, and where the Spirit of the Lord is, there is liberty. But we all, with unveiled face, beholding as in a mirror the glory of the Lord, are being transformed into the same image from glory to glory, just as from the Lord, the Spirit.
2 Corinthians 3:16-18

The enemy of your heart knows there are keys to your freedom. He also knows the Word of God, and the Word of God is clear that the ultimate key to your freedom is the Holy Spirit. We can't start this process to freedom and healing without the One who has the ability to bring it forth.

Now the Lord is the Spirit, and where the Spirit of the Lord is, there is freedom.
2 Corinthians 3:17

I wrestled with whether I should embrace this topic first or last, uncertain of how it would be received, knowing how deeply deceived I personally was about the Holy Spirit. I also know that without this discussion first, the work we do following will be unfruitful. There is a reason why the Word says the Spirit brings freedom, and we certainly can't expect to find freedom without Him, though most of us probably can admit we have certainly tried. My experience speaking to women is that women are hungry for truth, so I am praying you are hungry enough to receive this with an open heart.

My personal story is that I was raised with tremendous fear surrounding the subject of the gifts of the Holy Spirit. Yes, I believed that I received the Holy Spirit when I was baptized as a young girl, but because far too many had abused the gifts of the Spirit making them more 'weird' than desirable, I never pursued a life with the Spirit or gifts of the Spirit. Out of desperation for something *more* and *real*, I began to passionately seek truth, and I was led to the calling of Paul:

Follow the way of love and eagerly desire gifts of the Spirit, especially prophecy.
1 Corinthians 14:1

Tragically, I believe many people in the church today are like I was — completely blinded to the power of the Holy Spirit. I find there are three reasons we are missing what Jesus calls His gift: First, some people abused the Holy Spirit and made it "weird" and thus created fear around it. Second, tradition rather than scripture said that the Holy Spirit didn't work for believers today as it did in our History of faith, so it was ultimately quenched in many believers. Lastly, people had no experience to disprove tradition, so they chose to be comfortable in their beliefs rather than to be stretched to find their own truth.

I was guilty of all three. I had tremendous fear surrounding the Holy Spirit, especially because I was a people pleasing perfectionist and heaven forbid the Spirit make me look "weird." I had seen and heard of it's abuse and I wanted nothing to do with it. I now realize how strategic this lie is. You need to know the enemy loves to twist and pervert the very things that he knows will awaken you, free you, and unleash you so that you will miss the blessings of God. Satan wants nothing more than to keep you deceived. The spirit of God does NOT make us weird. The spirit of God brings us freedom and intimacy, and your enemy fears you finding both. Thus, he uses fear to keep you from the very key to the Kingdom of God.

Additionally, there were people in my life that were leaders and even Pastors that made claims that what I received from the Holy Spirit at baptism was all that I needed, so I thought I had it all. Instead of pursuing more of what God offered, I fulfilled my Christian obligation to attend church, read my Bible, and serve in all of the ways I believed guaranteed my salvation.

Unfortunately, I received my truth from men that denied the power, instead of pursuing an experience to match God's *all powerful* Word. When my heart longed for more, I began to look out for the world to meet this longing instead of up to God, because I believed I had all there was of Jesus. However, my life was full, but my soul was so empty and I was completely deceived at the depth of my own bondage. Ultimately, at the bottom, I was forced to look up, and in looking up I found truth that there was so much more to the life Jesus offered than what I had been taught. I say this in love, but sweet friend, you must know the truth is that this teaching, "all that you have of the Holy Spirit at baptism is all you need," comes against the Word of God. Luke 11 clearly leads us to ask and keep asking, seek and keep seeking, and knock and keep knocking for the gift of the Holy Spirit.

So I say to you: Ask and it will be given to you; seek and you will find; knock and the door will be opened to you. For everyone who asks receives; the one who seeks finds; and to the one who knocks, the door will be opened. Which of you

fathers, if your son asks for a fish, will give him a
snake instead? Or if he asks for an egg, will give
him a scorpion? If you then, though you are evil,
know how to give good gifts to your children,
how much more will your Father in heaven give
the Holy Spirit to those who ask him!
Luke 11:9-13

The Holy Spirit —a concept that has had so much fear built around it— is actually a gift from God. There are at least fifty scriptures that speak to what the Holy Spirit does in our lives, and while we won't explore them all in this chapter, I will encourage you to search scripture for yourself to see all that is available through this gift. The Holy Spirit frees us, remodels us, regenerates us, comforts us, teaches us, guides us into truth, reveals the deeper things of God, and the list goes on. Without the Holy Spirit we have an empty Christian experience, because it is through this Spirit that we have access to the Father[16.] God's desire is not that you know *about* Him, but that you have communion *with* Him. We can't do this without the power of the Holy Spirit that gives us that access. This is what you have been missing if you have been searching for more, and believe like I did—that the Holy Spirit isn't necessary to an abundant life in Christ.

The truth is that the enemy of your heart is not a little red man with a pitch fork as so many have depicted, but rather the Word says he is a master imitator of God who can come like a lion[17], and he can also come like the light[18]. I believe today we see this 'light' often in churches in the form of tradition. It can appear to be 'good' and such a part of our church DNA that we are completely blinded to the fact that it doesn't align to truth. There are so many in our churches deceived by tradition much like the Pharisees in the days of Jesus. The Pharisees were the 'religious people' that should have recognized Him first, yet they missed Him completely. We can read scripture and see how obviously deceived they were, and yet be blinded to our own deception. Don't allow law or tradition to override His truth and keep you from His inheritance.

I want you to ponder the Words of Jesus...

But very truly I tell you, it is for your good that I am going away. Unless I go away, the Advocate will not come to you; but if I go, I will send him to you. John 16:7

I have had the amazing privilege of walking in the Holy Land. This place now holds a huge part of my heart. I had no idea how connected I would be to His land and His people there. I live with a longing to return. I can't imagine Jesus living here and now, in this moment, and getting to walk with Him as His disciples did. Can you imagine watching as He turned water into wine and raised the dead and delivered those tormented with disease and demons? I can't even put language to how it must have been to walk with Him, physically holding His hand, yet He says, "It is better for you that I go." Why? Don't miss this: It is better that He goes, so that He can send the Advocate or Comforter. By Him leaving, He is able to send the teacher and the transformer, so that every person that believes can feel like the twelve disciples that walked with Him. We too would have intimate relationship with Jesus through the Holy Spirit, and along with this gift would come a life empowered to replicate the life of Jesus here on Earth.

Today, more believers than not have choked out the seed that would give us the power to live out the great commission. There is NO scripture that defends this modern day notion that God stopped operating in this day and age as He did in our History, but a lack of experience has led most people to assume that He has. If you are deeply embedded in this lie and need to walk through the scripture with greater understanding, as I did, the best foundational, scriptural teaching I have found is *The God I Never Knew* by Robert Morris. I highly encourage you to watch this series at www.theblessedlife.com in conjunction with reading this book, because we can't expect to be free, if we have fear around the key to that freedom.

God has called me to lead people to an experience with the one true living God that will wreck the toxic theology that has led to the death of far too many churches across our nation. I am not asking you to revolt against a church or a teacher or to leave your faith, but rather to recognize that we all have one enemy who has deceived the masses for far too long. I believe as you get free, you will be the flame that lights revival right where you are.

People encountered Jesus and it altered their life courses. It is our history. It is my story. And if you have not had an encounter with Jesus that has altered your path, then I am believing you will have it here as press in seeking truth. I even believe we were called to take it a step further allowing our encounter with Him, to empower us to awaken others to His Kingdom on Earth. In essence, people would have encounters with us that would alter their life courses and awaken them to truth, as well.

We will talk more about the cultural faith that doesn't align to Jesus, but for this day I want us to open our hearts to the Holy Spirit.

PRAYER

Father, we come before Your throne of mercy today, and we repent for everything that we have spoken against or believed about Your gift of the Holy Spirit that violates Your Word. Your Word is our source of truth. We will not allow the lack of an experience to keep us from what You long to do through us this day in time. You chose *us* to live in this moment of history. You have given us voices to release influence over our communities and our nation. We need to be empowered by Your Holy Spirit. We need You to fill us beyond measure with Your Holy Spirit. We need, more than anything, to come close to Your heart, and we recognize today that it is through the power of the Holy Spirit that we draw near. We renounce every assignment on our lives for agreeing with the enemy of our soul and quenching Your Spirit. We plead the blood of Jesus over our lives and every lie spoken, and we receive Your forgiveness that is so fully available. Father, Your Word says that if we ask, seek, and knock that you being a Good Father would give us the gift of the

Holy Spirit[19], so today we come and lay at your feet and ask for this gift. Father will you open our hearts to more? Will you open our spiritual ears? Will you open the eyes of our hearts? Will you give us wisdom and revelation to know You? We come before You thirsty, and we ask that You let us experience what it is to drink deeply.

In the name of Jesus,
Amen

He speaks to my heart...

Do you have fear around the Holy Spirit? Give your fear to Jesus. Your heart is safe with Him. Ask Him to speak.

_____

_____

_____

_____

_____

_____

_____

_____

_____

_____

_____

_____

CHAPTER FOUR:

The American Gospel

This is eternal life that you know me.
John 17:3

I call the version of Jesus that we as Americans tend to buy into "The American Gospel." It is comfortable, responsible, palatable, and commendable. We attend church, wear a cross, and participate in Bible Study. We probably donate our tired items to charity and raise funds for missions. We are driven by doing good and avoiding evil. Our actions are more often motivated by fear of missing heaven or disappointing God, rather than compelled by a love that organically spills out from having tapped into living water.

The truth is that many of us are sadly misinformed, because none of these actions make us believers. We can sit on a pew for our entire life, and still miss eternal life. Recall the words of John 17:3, "This is eternal life, that you *know* me." God doesn't want your knowledge, service, participation, or attendance more than He wants your heart. His desire is that you *know* Him, not read about Him or hear about Him, but *know* Him

—spend *time* with Him. There is a bitter sweetness in my heart over the number of women that I have led, for the very first time, to experience an encounter with Jesus. What a tremendous blessing to get to be a part of that moment when they realize that He speaks, or they can experience His love, or see His face, or taste His goodness, but what a tragedy that so many have spent their whole lives in church without revelation of His presence. They never had a *real* encounter with God.

And when you seek with your whole heart, I will be found and bring you back from captivity.
Jeremiah 29:13

I have learned from my experience that captives can be imprisoned unaware. Many Christian leaders say that 60-80% are sitting in churches deceived, believing they have the full "Christian experience." And because they think they have their "God card" checked, when the longing for something MORE arises, they look vertically to meet those needs through roles, status, possessions, and relationships rather than looking up to the only one that can meet the deepest longings of their souls. This "American Gospel" keeps people comfortable rather than spurring them to look like Jesus.

This version of Christianity has also put a God of exceedingly, abundantly, above all into the proverbial box, and often leads people to criticize those that have let Him out. In essence, it looks very familiar to the days of Jesus where the 'scholars' rejected Him, so He chose to unleash His Kingdom through those they deemed disqualified. And ultimately as hard as it is to even conceive, not only did those who should have seen Him reject Him, but they also played a pivotal role in their Savior's crucifixion.

To truly follow Jesus today goes against the American culture. It calls for people of a different, set apart spirit much like Joshua, Caleb, and our beloved Esther. I don't know about you, but I desire to look different from this culture. I desire to dwell in the promised land rather than continue wandering in a wilderness just getting by on spiritual crumbs when He offers a feast. Sweet friends, we must desire truth in our innermost beings[20], not only to feast, but because our eternity depends on it. I feel such an urgency in my spirit as the words grow louder and louder....*Speak truth Rochelle, because My people are perishing for a lack of knowledge[21]*.

So let's look at what our culture embeds in us versus what is His TRUTH!

Our culture drives us to perform, possess, and acquire, yet the Word says, *You find your life when you lose it[22],*and *It is more blessed to give than receive[23].* Our culture encourages us to be comfortable, responsible, and fit in with the "crowd," yet the Word says, *The path that leads to life is narrow, and few find it[24].* Our culture tells us NOT to get our hopes up, yet the Word says, *Hope is the anchor for the soul that takes us behind the veil[25].* Our culture has driven families to spend their lives at ballfields, and led churches to shift schedules in certain seasons to accommodate the absence of those families, yet the Word says, *There are to be no idols before me[26].*

Our culture embeds in families certain traditions that outweigh the voice of God, and are often not even based on biblical principles. Our culture esteems a busy mom, yet Jesus said, Mary, at His feet, had chosen best. Our culture would say that real men don't cry, yet the Word is full of men who cried out to The Lord, and history reveals that men, moved to tears, led to most revivals. The culture would make you believe that attending church makes you a Christian, but the Word says, "Deny yourself, take up your cross and follow me![27]" The culture would tell us that we are to tolerate everything in an effort to show love, but the Word says, *Speak the truth in love!*[28]

It is easy to see how far the current culture has shifted from the knowledge and truth of God's ways. We've bought into an "American Gospel" that has wandered so far from the truth that our culture looks much like the Israelites, wandering in the wilderness, making false gods out of anything they felt like worshipping. It is vital that we detox some of our beliefs that don't align to the Word of God, because these beliefs may be hindering our ability to experience intimacy which brings the healing and freedom we so desperately need today.

Take some time to reflect on your own beliefs that may not align to God's Word. Review the areas I mentioned above and see if the Spirit convicts you to explore any deeper. Remember the Spirit convicts us, but does not condemn us. This exercise is not to bring on guilt, shame, or blame, but rather to awaken us to truth.

Therefore, there is now no condemnation for those who are in Christ Jesus.
Romans 8:1

Ask the Holy Spirit to show you areas where you may have bought into the American version of the Gospel?

_____

_____

_____

_____

_____

_____

_____

Repent for these beliefs and ask the Father to re-align you to His truth.

If we have made vows or believed lies that God can't move in certain ways, it hinders us from experiencing Him in that way. In realizing I made a lot of vows against the way God moves, speaks, and reveals Himself, I had to do a blanket prayer to cover all the careless words spoken in the bulk of my life where I thought I could see truth, yet I had no vision. Have you limited how God can move in your life?

_____

_____

_____

PRAYER

Father, I realize that I have limited what You can do in my life by vows and lies that do not align to Your truth. I repent, in the name of Jesus, for everything that I have spoken or believed that is not aligned to Your truth. I now plead the blood of Jesus over every word I have spoken or belief that I have had that comes against Your truth. I ask You, Father, to release fear in me that would hinder me from experiencing You in any way. Awaken my spirit from sleep, slumber, and complacency and allow my heart to be open to Your truth. If there is anything specifically that I need to repent for that is hindering me from experiencing you, please make it known to me now…

_____

_____

_____

_____

_____

_____

_____

_____

_____

_____

{Dismantle anything He shows you using The Five Rs.}
Recognize the Lie.
Repent for the Lie.
Renounce the Lie.
Receive His truth.
Replace the Lie with His truth.

He speaks to my heart...

Are you tired? Worn out? Burned out on religion? Come to
me. Get away with me and you'll recover your life.
Matthew 11: 28 MSG

_____

_____

_____

_____

_____

_____

_____

_____

_____

_____

_____

_____

_____

_____

_____

CHAPTER FIVE:

Realigning To The Kingdom

Jesus didn't die to make you comfortable.
He died to make you dangerous to the kingdom of darkness.
Christine Caine

The American Gospel can lead us to believe that to follow Jesus we attend church, make a profession of faith, walk an aisle, and get baptized and then live a "good" life until the glory bus arrives to usher us in to heaven. Though this process is revered in many churches it is nowhere in scripture. In the Jewish culture, when people confessed that Jesus was Lord, they often lost their families, homes, and careers. On our visit to the Holy Land in 2016, we had the opportunity to meet with what they called "Living Stones." These are people that have encountered Jesus today, and have converted from either Judaism or Islam. After hearing their stories of conversion, it was evident that the price of confessing Jesus as Lord still remains costly in other cultures, unlike our American experience. Professing that Jesus is Lord costs many people their lives and many more their lives as they know it, and these same people that are paying a price today live in the culture where the words were instructed over 2000 years ago:

If you declare with your mouth, "Jesus is Lord," and believe in your heart that God raised him from the dead, you will be saved.
Romans 10:9

The deception in the modern day church around the role of the church runs deep, and can be attributed to the condition of our nation that has gone morally blind and left the masses imprisoned to the very things Jesus died to free us from. It is dangerous to bank our faith on scripture from a culture and context that we don't understand, and according to the Jewish culture there has always been a price for following Jesus. We were *never* designed to get saved, check off our God boxes on our 'Heavenly To Do list,' and wait on a 'glory bus' that delivers us perfectly to the pearly gates of Heaven. We were created to be carriers of the Kingdom of Heaven on Earth. Tragically, too many churches are not modeling the teachings of Jesus:

And Jesus went about all Galilee, teaching in their synagogues, and preaching the gospel of the kingdom, and healing all manner of sickness and all manner of disease among the people.
Matthew 4:23

Jesus preached the Gospel of the Kingdom, and people were healed, delivered, and set free. Too many denominations today aren't teaching what Jesus taught, and we have churches full of what I call cisterns needing to be refilled every Sunday, instead of wells that have learned to tap into the source of living water as Jesus called us to do.

As followers of Jesus, we have to understand this Kingdom, because it was the core of His teaching. This Kingdom is not only when we die, but He says...

The Kingdom of Heaven is within you! Luke 17:21 KJV

The Kingdom of Heaven has come near.
Matthew 3:2, Mark 1:15, Luke 10:9

Freely you receive this {Kingdom}, now freely give it.
Matthew 10:8

Pray thy Kingdom Come on Earth as it is in Heaven.
Matthew 6:10

As I watched the women come day and night to the Western Wall in Jerusalem, I had an awakening to this truth that the Kingdom is now in us. As I approached the wall, a spirit of conviction hit me and I fell to my knees in tears. You see, day after day these people come to this wall offering up their prayers through tears at this wall, believing that their "way" to the presence of God is now blocked by Muslims. In their mind, the holy of holies is now buried in the mountain somewhere behind that wall. They even have a tour underground that they believe takes you to the closest place one can get to that presence, and even at 11pm we found women there crying out to God.

Yes, you can feel the presence of God in that holy place, but what they have missed and sadly many Christians do too, is that *we* are now the carries of the Kingdom. The sacred place is no longer in the Ark of the Covenant, but inside of us. *We* are the temple. This is why there is an intense battle over your identity, because when you realize who you are and what you possess everything changes! We have been *longing* and looking horizontally for answers and identity and worth, when all along the answer has been inside of us! If only we can just *be still*, and find that Secret Place where He is known and who we are in Him becomes our reality.

YOUR ASSIGNMENT:
Listen to worship music or instrumental worship music, if that helps you relax or connect to the Father.

Still yourself by meditating on the words,

Be still and know that I am God. Psalm 46:10

The Word says:
"We enter the gate with thanksgiving and into the courts with praise," Psalm 100

Spend a few minutes thanking God and praising His name while imagining yourself entering the gate to your heart. Invite Jesus to show you the Kingdom inside of you.

PRAYER
{Make this prayer fit to your truth.}

Father, I recognize that I have believed and lived from a lie that....*Your Kingdom of Heaven was only available when I left this earth* or *I believed a lie that I wasn't worthy of carrying Your Kingdom on earth.* I renounce this lie and I repent for my complacency that has kept me from Your Commissioning to bring forth Your Kingdom. I stand on Your truth today that THE KINGDOM OF HEAVEN IS WITHIN IN ME! I choose to live from this truth. Father, I ask that You speak to my heart now and show me this Kingdom You have placed in my heart.

He speaks to my heart...

Spend some time today connecting with Jesus. Ask Him to show you the kingdom inside of you, and write every detail in your journal. Do you notice colors, or images, or objects? Ask Him to teach you how to connect with Him. What do you love about this time communing with Him?

_____

_____

_____

_____

_____

_____

_____

_____

_____

_____

_____

_____

_____

_____

_____

_____

CHAPTER SIX:

Striving: The Enemy of Intimacy

God's holy beauty comes near you, like a spiritual scent, and it stirs your drowsing soul...He creates in you the desire to find Him and run after Him- to follow wherever He leads you, and to press peacefully against His heart wherever He is.
John of the Cross

Our hearts long to be united to the heart of the Father, but it is only in stillness that we can come to fully understand the answer to this longing. We know the instructions by heart, but living them out is a different story. *Be still and know me [29]. This is eternal life that you know me[30].*

This call to stillness comes completely against a culture that would assure you that to be known you must perform. As we detox from the world, we will also detox from cultural beliefs that hinder our relationship with the Father, because everything else will flow from that relationship. When we *know* Him, it changes everything else in our lives. We live differently when we are connected to His love, we spend our money and time differently, we shift our passions and many of our relationships and even sometimes our career paths. We begin to see differently and more clearly, and the lines that once divided the body seem to wash away and are replaced with a longing to be united. It is beautiful how all of this seems to happen organically from the love of the Father. Knowing the power of this love, we must seek to remove the roadblocks to experiencing it.

One of the largest roadblocks that I have had to personally overcome was striving and performance. This need to perform or be seen to feel validated or worthy in our culture can bleed over into our spiritual journey, as well. Since our culture drives us to perform for promotion in the physical, we struggle with simply accepting that we are loved, chosen, and worthy completely from the actions of Jesus rather than our own personal performance. This struggle to perform is always birthed from impure motives. This doesn't mean that the motives are malicious or have any evil intent, but there is always something deeper than identity in Christ that drives us to perform for His approval. This is vital for us to understand, because God looks at our hearts[31].

TESTIMONY

Despite my pursuit to freedom, I was seeing remnants of performance rising up again. I asked the Holy Spirit to show me the root, because if we have dealt with something and it is still bearing fruit in our lives, then we haven't laid an axe to the root. As I was seeking to find stillness to hear Him, I recalled an emotionally tragic memory from my first year of elementary school. Unlike the other children in my class, I only attended one year of preschool. It was assumed that I wasn't prepared for first grade like the other children, so they placed me in a class with students that needed more help. All of my friends were in the class labeled as the "smarter children," and even at seven years old I began to feel the effects of rejection and comparison.

The first few weeks of school would begin to shake my identity. Even though I would not see this truth until I was in my forties, I wrestled with the fruit of it all of my life. I was embarrassed on the playground when our classes came together believing the other children looked at me as less than them, and I felt so left out sitting with the other class over lunch, longing to be invited to my friend's table.

So as a seven year old little girl, I decided that I would work harder than everyone else to prove that I indeed belonged in the other class. Within a few weeks, it was evident that I was too far ahead of my classmates, and I needed to be moved to the class with all of my friends. As you can see, striving entered the door at seven years old. I ended up graduating the top of my class evidently *still* trying to prove that I had value, because I was 'smart.'

When the Holy Spirit shows us a memory in a moment of seeking a root, we always need to ask, "Did I believe a lie here?" So, I asked the Holy Spirit: "Did I believe a lie in this moment of heartache and embarrassment?" Almost immediately, I heard that I believed I was unseen and overlooked. I then asked if I had made a vow as a result of this lie, and again quickly I heard, " I will have to work harder than others to be noticed and promoted."

There are times like this one where I hear the Holy Spirit very quickly, and other times where I must be still and wait—sometimes for days to hear specifically. Still there are other times, when I don't hear until someone says something days or weeks later that triggers a memory that leads to the vow. Usually if we have believed a lie, we have made a vow that prevents us, or we believe protects us, from experiencing the pain associated with the lie. For example: I don't ever want to feel overlooked and unseen, so I will work so hard to assure that I am not.

This particular vow had driven my life, even though I was only a seven year old little girl when I made it. It had driven me to performance in every area of my life. It was important that I dealt with the pain in my heart that began at seven years of age from being humiliated, ashamed, and left out. I had to invite the Holy Spirit into every part of this pain and allow myself to feel it one more time. Sometimes we must go back to our pain one more time to dismantle something that is driving us on the wrong course.

God isn't after a perfect performance—He is after your heart. Unfortunately, our culture breeds performers and promotes striving, so most of us, if not all of us, need to release this spirit that steals the intimacy that only comes from a place of surrender and stillness. If we believe that in our effort we can become worthy of His Presence, we have missed His Grace. God wants us fully leaning into, and dependent on, His Grace. There is nothing I can do or have done to be worthy of His presence, affection, or attention. I simply must receive the finished work of my Savior, Jesus Christ, and that finished work offers me a new life hidden in Christ.

I want you to ask the Holy Spirit to help you answer the next few questions in truth. Sometimes we are deceived that we have a struggle, so we ask the voice of truth to speak into our hearts today —specifically into this area of striving.

Do you find yourself needing to perform or stay busy to be seen or noticed or validated?

_____

_____

_____

Do you sense that you strive to find God or to be accepted by Him?

_____

_____

_____

Do you feel that you need to earn His approval?

_____

_____

_____

Do you feel God is disappointed with you when you aren't doing all that you "should" be doing as a Christian?

_____

_____

_____

If you sense that striving or performance are a pattern in your life, ask the Holy Spirit for the root. It is important that we uproot the vows and lies we have made and replace them with truth.

What was my root of performance and striving?

_____

_____

_____

_____

How old was I when I started this pattern?

_____

_____

_____

Is this the earliest memory of performance?

_____

_____

_____

If you see a memory, ask if you believed a lie?

_____

_____

_____

Did I make a vow as a result of this lie?

_____

_____

What is God's truth about this lie or vow?

_____

_____

_____

This step of replacing lies with truth is vital.

When an impure spirit comes out of a person, it goes through arid places seeking rest and does not find it. Then it says, 'I will return to the house I left.' When it arrives, it finds the house swept clean and put in order. Then it goes and takes seven other spirits more wicked than itself, and they go in and live there. And the final condition of that person is worse than the first."
Luke 11:24-26

We are ultimately 'cleaning house' on this journey together. We are removing what God has not intended to rest in our souls. The enemy *will* return, but if the truth has taken up residence, the enemy must flee.

{Dismantle the lie/vow by using The Five Rs.}

Recognize the Lie.
Repent for the Lie.
Renounce the Lie.
Receive His truth.
Replace the Lie with His truth.

He speaks to my heart...

Do not love the world or anything in the world. If anyone loves the world, love for the Father is not in them.
1 John 2:15

The culture calls us to conform, but the Word says we are to be different from the world. We don't need to keep the pace that our culture demands, but rather be still and find new direction.

_____
_____
_____
_____
_____
_____
_____
_____
_____
_____
_____
_____
_____
_____
_____
_____
_____
_____
_____
_____
_____
_____
_____

CHAPTER SEVEN:

The Source of Life

We can not attain the presence of God because we're
already totally in the presence of God.
What's absent is awareness.
Richard Rohr

One of the greatest teachings that shifted my spiritual growth came from Bob Hamp, formerly a Freedom Minister at Gateway Church in Dallas, Texas. His revelation involves the two trees in the garden of Eden. I know for me, I spent most of my life on one tree...the tree of Good and Evil. I tried with all that I had to stay on the GOOD side of this tree. I even praised myself at times for being "so good!" The problem with this thinking is that even though it is 'good,' it is still the wrong tree!

You see God created Adam and Eve to walk with Him, commune with Him, and depend on Him. He was their only source for their every need. He even gave them a tree of life where they could partake and eat of life. In eating from this tree, they stayed connected to God as their source. However, when they ate from the one forbidden tree, which held the knowledge of good and evil, they were not only choosing a new and different tree, but they were changing their source. God was no longer their source of life, deciding what they needed and did not need, but rather they would become their own source, choosing between good and evil.

In disconnecting from *His* source, they immediately took on the fruit of this new tree: guilt, shame, blame, and hiding. They began to self protect rather than submit to God. As a result of their disobedience to God, they were removed from the garden of fellowship where they had full access to their Creator and complete freedom. They would now live in a fallen condition between the temptations of choices that were considered good and evil, and this struggle would become a legacy to those of faith. Our desire as believers ultimately became to move ourselves and others from the evil side of the tree to the better side of the tree by behavior modification, doing good works, and striving to fulfill 'Christian obligations.'

The problem with this entanglement in the church today is that it was never meant for us to behave one way or another to find our worth. It was never intended for us to have the power to judge good vs evil. It was never intended for us to be removed from His presence. We were designed for intimate fellowship with the Father. Changing our source leads us to perform and to try to be 'good' to maintain our position on the 'good side' of the tree. In becoming our own source, we believe our provision and our promotion and even our path to Jesus is in our hands. He did give us free will right? Yes, He did give us free will, but He also gave us the option to hand that free will back, just as Jesus demonstrated when He said *not my will but thy will be done*[32].

Jesus also said that He came that we would have *life*[33]. So Jesus came as the Redeemer who would restore us back to the source of life! This is *so* good! In essence, we get to go back to the garden where we have complete access to walk and talk with the Father, because the death on one tree redeemed the curse brought from the other.

Let's recap this thought.

There were two trees specifically mentioned in the Garden of Eden: The Tree of Life and The Tree of the Knowledge of Good & Evil. One tree kept Adam and Eve in fellowship with God where He was their source of life. They could freely partake from this tree. The other forbidden tree offered them knowledge of good and evil, but it came with disconnection from the Source of life. They were warned that if they ate from this forbidden tree that they would die. Eating the forbidden fruit caused spiritual death and separation. Then Jesus came offering….. to give us LIFE back.

I came that you would have life, and have it abundantly. John 10:10

What Jesus was offering, was to connect us back to our Source of life. He was not simply trying to change our behavior to the better side of the wrong tree. Many of us work hard everyday, striving to be good enough, trying to finish our heavenly to do list, filling our days with "doing good" when what God wants most from us is our attention and intimate relationship with Him as our source. Yes, I know you need to marinate in this and I pray you do, because this truth alone will free many of you from a life driven to live up to something you never can!

ACTIVATION:

Ask your Father to show you where you have become your own source. God doesn't want some areas of your life while you hold on to the rest. He wants *every* area of your life. Is He your source of provision? Your source of love? Your source of Protection? Your source of Identity? Your source of freedom?

Are you looking for someone or something to be what only God desires to be for you? {Career, Roles, Status, Relationships, Possessions, Food, Knowledge and Money can all be the wrong source, but when God becomes our ultimate source, all of these areas of our lives can be restored.}

Are you on the good side of the wrong tree like I was? I will admit that I grieved after hearing this teaching, because my life was completely planted on the wrong tree. I was striving to provide for my family, because I believed I was our only source. I had the fruit of success, so it looked good to others, and I esteemed myself, yet when the mask came off, I was empty. I was looking for validation and identity from promotions and rewards at my pharmaceutical company rather than from being a child of God. Again, I was the source rather than Him. Is there really *anything* we should desire more than to be called His daughter? {Think about that for a moment…Is there anything we should desire more than to be called His daughter?} I had a tree filled with some really alluring fruit of the world, but no evidence of an intimate relationship with the Creator of the universe that I have the privilege of calling Father, and little or possibly no fruit of the Kingdom.

Are you trying to be "good" more than in relationship?

_____

_____

_____

_____

Recognize where you have bought into a lie that being or doing "good" makes you a Christian. Repent from believing that lie. Renounce any assignments on your life for coming into agreement with that lie. Receive truth from the Holy Spirit and replace the lie with truth.

Galatians 5:22-23 says:
But the fruit of the Spirit is love, joy, peace, forbearance, kindness, goodness, faithfulness, gentleness and self-control. Against such things there is no law.

If you recall in the garden there was no law, except to not partake in the fruit of one forbidden tree. So the fruit of one who has shifted back to the source of life—the correct tree—should look like the fruit of the Spirit...love, joy, peace, patience, kindness, goodness, faithfulness, gentleness, and self-control.

This fruit is priceless! Does your life produce this kind of fruit? Why or why not?

_____

_____

_____

_____

_____

To Note: If we have the Spirit of God in us, it should be evidenced by fruit. This fruit we don't have to ask for, but rather begin to manifest. The fruit is within you, so be prolific!

He speaks to my heart...

He desires intimacy more than striving.
He desires your connection more than your good works.
He desires your heart more than your resume.
Are you willing to shift trees?

_____

_____

_____

_____

_____

_____

_____

_____

_____

_____

_____

_____

_____

_____

_____

_____

_____

_____

_____

SECTION TWO:

Restore
My
Soul

CHAPTER EIGHT:

The Assignment on Your Heart

Create in me a pure heart, O God, and
renew a steadfast spirit within me.
Psalm 51:10

There was a season when I was truly struggling with a broken, battered, and abused heart. I felt like it had just been ripped into a million pieces. As a result of my pain, I erected a fortress that would keep myself protected. I was becoming numb and distrusting as my belief began to agree with the world that had taught me to stuff my emotions and use my head instead. I would grow in wisdom and independence rather than be weak and vulnerable.

The problem here is that in my effort to protect my wounded heart by keeping out the "bad," I also kept out the only answer to my pain — the love of God. I allowed my heart to be rooted in lies that now opened my mind up to torment, rather than truth that leads to freedom. Out of desperation to get free, God gave me this revelation that softened my heart, and allowed my interior walls to surrender to His perfect love.

I would be remiss if I did not speak this into your life, knowing the healing it brought to my own.

The enemy is fiercely after the heart of a woman. He approaches a woman differently than He does a man, because we are wired differently than men. He knows first that we operate organically from our hearts, so if he can wound our heart, he can ultimately take our vision, our treasure, our voice, our love, our blessing, our hope, our calling, our identity,our life source, our trust, and our belief.

Ponder these scriptures:

God looks at your heart.
1 Samuel 16:7

If you BELIEVE with your heart, you will be saved.
Romans 10:9

As you THINK in your heart so are you.
Proverbs 23:7

Open the EYES of your heart so that you can see His hope and calling.
Ephesians 1:18

Your treasure is in your heart.
Matthew 6: 21.

He poured HIS LOVE in your hearts.
Romans 5:5

Out of the abundance of the heart the mouth
SPEAKS.
Luke 6:45

He set ETERNITY in your hearts.
Ecclesiastes 3:11

BLESSED are the pure in heart for they will see God.
Matthew 5:8

TRUST with your heart.
Proverbs 3:5-6

Perhaps this is why the Word also says...

Guard your heart above all else, for it determines the course of your life. Proverbs 4:23

The culture would tell you that operating from your heart is weak, but the Word would tell you that your heart is a prime piece of real-estate, and even more so when you understand the influence of a woman's voice. I believe the assignment on the heart of the woman goes back to the Garden of Eden.

First: The enemy knows you have influence. The serpent went to the woman to eat first, knowing she had influence as Adam's bride. Despite the authority of the garden given to Adam, he chose to obey his wife rather than God and eat from the only restriction in the garden. We see in scripture a pattern of women influencing their husbands decisions, like in the example of Sarah and Abraham. Despite the promise of the Lord to Abraham that Sarah would have his child, Sarah disbelieving sent him to sleep with her maidservant to assure the vision of their life was fulfilled. {In case you missed it, she was her source!} Strangely enough, Abraham does as his bride advises. We see it with Bathsheba and David, when she petitions him to name Solomon as King, and he also sees to his wife's wishes. We see it when Esther comes before her pagan husband to save her people despite a law that would demand her life be taken for such dishonor. The influence of women is consistent throughout scripture. **These women had intimacy with their husbands, identity as their brides, and they had influence over their circumstances.**

Second: The curse after the fall states that there would be enmity between serpent and woman. It does not say this about man, but solely there would be a deep seeded hatred that leads to violence or enmity between the woman and Satan. He comes fiercely to halt your destiny, knowing the power a woman who steps into her true identity. We, as women, have this same enmity back toward him, so when we get free we make him pay a great price for the years we missed deceived by his schemes. It wasn't enough that I began to walk in freedom, but I had to lead as many women to freedom as I could. In the words of Lisa Bevere, I became "dangerously awake!"

Third: The other part of the curse is that our seed would crush his head. While this was referring to the seed of Jesus from Mary crushing the enemy and restoring us back to authority and intimacy, Luke 8:11 also say that the Word is also seed. When we realize the power of our voice and speak in alignment to the Word, we have the ability to shift atmospheres and call forth the Kingdom of God on earth. Your enemy knows this truth. He knows the power of your voice. He also knows that if he can wound you in the heart, he can take your voice. Knowing this, his strategy has been to use those that matter most to wound you deepest to render you voiceless. Specifically he uses men, because he knows our longing for love and acceptance. So he will use a high school rejection, an absent father, a betrayal of a husband, abuse, or emotional trauma to cause your heart to callous and become numb, so you feel unworthy or disqualified to speak.

I want you to take in this truth: You have one enemy. It is none of the men that hurt you, even though the pain is deep and the wickedness that you have experienced was never the desire of the Father. The enemy of your heart uses vessels to fulfill his purpose. I know there were things like rejection or betrayal that I held on to for twenty years, though the people that caused those emotions probably had no idea that I still carried them twenty years later. The enemy, however, never let me forget, and reminded me—sometimes daily— of the rejection and pain, knowing that if I could grow numb and distrusting it would steal the power of my voice, and also separate me from the life of God as Ephesians 4:18 speaks:

They are darkened in their understanding and separated from the life of God because of a hardened heart.

There has to come a point where we want freedom from our past, and a passion to live out our destiny, more than we need others to pay for our pain. To embrace the life God calls us to, hardened hearts must heal.

There is a parable of a man who owed a great debt.[34] The master, however, cleared his debt. This same man that is freed from debt holds another man accountable for a smaller debt. The parable says that this angered the master, so he handed the man he had freed over to the tormentors. This story is a picture of what withholding forgiveness does to our minds. When we choose to hold on to something toxic, we open ourselves up to torment. If we truly grasp the price that Jesus paid to free us, we have to be willing to free everyone that has abused, offended, betrayed, and rejected our broken little hearts. It is the way of Jesus to release. When you can understand that the person who wounded you most, was simply influenced by the enemy of your heart, it is easier to release.

For we wrestle not against flesh and blood, but against principalities, against powers, against the rulers of the darkness of this world, against spiritual wickedness in high places.
Ephesians 6:12

It is time that we find our voices, but to find them we must access the condition of our hearts that will bring forth our voices of influence.

ACTIVATION

What is the condition of your heart? Is it bandaged, damaged, wounded, ripped, gushing, bruised, aching, grieving or empty? Is it whole or hiding? We are taught in our culture to stuff, but stuffing only works when we aren't in relationships. When we begin to connect with others again, inevitably our 'stuff' comes out, and often our 'stuff' isn't pretty. This same 'stuff' will hinder our relationships both horizontally and vertically.

_____

_____

_____

_____

Ask the Father to show you your heart. Close your eyes and connect to your heart. {I prefer to listen to instrumental worship music to move to a place of stillness.} You may want to repeat these words to set your heart with His:

Be still and know that I am God.
Be still and know that I am.
Be still and know me.
Be still and know.
Be still.
Be.

1.) What is the condition of your heart?

_____

_____

_____

2.) Ask Him to show you what it was that damaged or wounded your heart?

_____

_____

_____

_____

3.) Where did the_____{ Wound, Damage, Grief} come from?

_____

_____

_____

_____

4.) How did you feel in this moment?

_____

_____

_____

_____

5.) Have you found a coping mechanism that you use to prevent your heart from experiencing this pain again?

_____

_____

_____

_____

6.) Did you believe a lie or make a vow due to this circumstance?

_____

_____

_____

_____

7.) Who do you need to forgive for tempting you to believe this vow or lie?

_____

_____

_____

_____

8.) Dismantle the lie or vow

Recognize it isn't of God.
Repent for agreeing with the lie.
Renounce any assignments attached to the lie.
Receive the truth from the Father.
Replace the lie with truth.

9.) Ask the Holy Spirit to release the wound, pain, bondage and replace it with His love.

I recommend listening to a song that speaks to the love of the Father while you visualize yourself receiving the love of the Father moving from your head, through your heart, and to your feet.

Song Suggestions:
"Lord I'm Amazed By You" by Steffany Gretzinger
"This Love" by Housefires
"Once and For All" by Lauren Daigle
"What Love Is This" by Kari Jobe
"Blameless" by Dara Mclean

You have one enemy. He fears the voice that comes from your heart, so he uses those that can hurt you the most to wound you deeply, rendering your heart ineffective. When the enemy of your heart seeks to shatter it, remember:

The Lord is close to the brokenhearted
and saves those who are crushed in spirit.[35]

He speaks to my heart...

Can you trust that your heart is safe with Jesus? Can you lean into the One that promises that He is closest in the midst of your trials and heartaches?

_____

_____

_____

_____

_____

_____

_____

_____

_____

_____

_____

_____

_____

_____

_____

_____

_____

_____

_____

_____

_____

_____

CHAPTER NINE:

A Sick Heart

Hope deferred makes the heart sick,
but a longing fulfilled is a tree of life.
Proverbs 13:12

How often have we heard these words, "Don't get your hopes up?" These words appear safe and non-threatening. They even seem aligned to guarding your heart, right? Don't allow yourself to live in disappointment because you know what that has done to your heart in the past, right? This seemingly simple statement is far more dangerous than we realize. The truth is that in partnering with this lie that steals your hope, you give birth to doubt. According to James, doubt leads us to double mindedness and instability.

If any of you lacks wisdom, you should ask God,
who gives generously to all without finding fault,
and it will be given to you. But when you ask, you
must believe and not doubt, because the one who
doubts is like a wave of the sea, blown and tossed

by the wind. That person should not expect to re-
ceive anything from the Lord. Such a person is
double-minded and unstable in all they do.
James 1:5-8

According to this passage, what should a person with doubt expect from God?

_____

Isn't it interesting that the very thing you think may be protecting your heart, is actually blocking exactly what your heart needs? Hope could actually be the key that unlocks the door to your breakthrough.

Proverbs 13:12 says: Hope deferred makes a heart sick, but a longing fulfilled becomes a

_____.

Hebrews 6:19-20 says, "We have this Hope as an _____ for the soul, firm and secure. It enters the inner sanctuary behind the curtain, where our forerunner, Jesus, has entered on our behalf. "

According to the world, hope will only leave you disappointed, but according to the Word, hope met transforms your sick hearts into a tree of life, hope is the anchor for your souls, and hope is what takes us into the presence of God behind the veil that once separated us from Him.

So the enemy would have you believe a lie that you shouldn't get your hopes up because you will end up disappointed, when in truth it is hope that grants you access into the secret place with God.

For now we see in a mirror dimly, but then face to face; now I know in part, but then I will know fully just as I also have been fully known. But now faith, hope, love, abide these three; but the greatest of these is love.
1 Corinthians 13:12-13

It is time to realign to His truth and get your HOPES up! Graham Cooke says, "Doubt attracts attacks," and you have lived as easy prey long enough, so let's go to the root of disappointment that has given doubt reign in your life.

Ask the Holy Spirit to show you if you have allowed doubt or disappointment in your heart?

_____

_____

_____

_____

_____

Where did doubt enter into your life?

_____

_____

_____

Have you agreed with the lie that you shouldn't get your hopes up?

_____

_____

_____

_____

Who has disappointed you in the past? How?

_____

_____

_____

_____

_____

Ask the Father to help you forgive anyone who tempted you to live without hope.

_____

_____

_____

Are there any desires that you have given up due to fear of disappointment?

_____

_____

_____

Ask the Father to reignite the desires of your heart that have been quenched by fear. Father, bring to remembrance what I have hidden in my heart.

_____

_____

_____

_____

If you recognize that you have believed any other lies in this process, make sure you dismantle them as well using The Five Rs:

Recognize the Lie.
Repent for the Lie.
Renounce the Lie.
Receive His truth.
Replace the Lie with His truth.

He speaks to my heart...

A longing fulfilled becomes a tree of life. So think about this…God wants to reconnect us to the tree of life and then make our lives a tree of life. As we live out what He put in our hearts, people will feast on our fruits and partake in life.

_____

_____

_____

_____

_____

_____

_____

_____

_____

_____

_____

_____

_____

_____

_____

_____

_____

_____

_____

_____

_____

CHAPTER TEN:

An Orphan Spirit

The Spirit you received does not make you slaves,
so that you live in fear again; rather, the Spirit you received
brought about your adoption to sonship. And by him
we cry, "Abba, Father."
Romans 8:15

I love the story of Esther for so many reasons, but probably most because my heart strings are always pulled at the thought of the orphan becoming the queen. It is our Biblical "Cinderella Story" that just captivates the heart of every woman, right? We long to be the bride and the princess and the chosen one, and Esther just brings them all together in a way that even causes our hearts to skip a beat at the sound of her name. Could we all have that moment....*For Such A Time As This!*

As I have studied Esther, I have felt that there was so much more to her story than a Jewish orphan girl saving her people. I do believe it is *our* story. I believe it is every woman's story of feeling like we don't belong, or we aren't worthy, or we are alone like orphans until we encounter Jesus. This encounter....our night with our King, if you will, moves us from orphan spirit to daughter, heir, bride!

Women today are in identity crisis like never before, and it appears from my traveling to all four corners of this country speaking to church women, that church women are just as much in identity crisis as women "lost" in the world. "I am not enough" and "I am alone" are spirits that have taken hold of most women today, even many of those serving in ministry. The enemy of your heart knows that you are an heir. The enemy knows you are a bride and your price has been paid, and he is making every attempt to keep you bound as an orphan so you never fully step into your true identity.

We must release this orphan spirit and receive a spirit of adoption that God offers. We are no longer slaves, but we are children of God. What I have found is that this spirit is not one that simply is released through a prayer {though I believe God can do that}, but rather this is a mindset change that requires intentionally taking the toxic thoughts that bind us to this spirit captive, and making them obedient to God's truth. We must renew our minds, so that we live from the mind of Christ and the identity and belonging that is found there. This spirit is also released as you come into a fuller revelation of the love of the Father.

Some Symptoms of the Orphan Spirit
I often feel like I don't belong, even with family.
I struggle with fear, insecurity, and anxiety.
I am independent and I don't need help.
I am often concerned with provision.
I feel unprotected and uncovered.
I have feelings of abandonment, loneliness, alienation, and rejection.
I am in survival mode often.
I follow the rules not to upset authority and lose my protection.
I perform to feel validated.
My identity comes from being better than others, so I have inner competition or turmoil
My identity is in things or titles.

You can have great parents and still struggle with the orphan spirit, because most people carry symptoms of this spirit, despite their upbringing. I believe this spirit comes from the removal of Adam and Eve from the garden. In no longer belonging in our original place, our DNA began to carry a sense of being alienated. The effects of the removal from the garden coupled with the desire to live on the "good side" of the tree {refer to The Source of Life}, created a perfect partnership to begin to manifest this orphan spirit. Add to this mixture a high school rejection, a friendship betrayal, an absent parent, a moment of fear, and a history of being overlooked, and you can see why this spirit is embedded in us so deeply.

Not to mention that you have an enemy that knows the power of you coming into agreement with what the word of God says about you.

For the creation waits in eager expectation for the children of God to be revealed
Romans 8:19

Creation *longs* for you to step into who you are.

As I mentioned earlier, this is a mindset change that calls for us to do our part in renewing of our mind and taking our thoughts captive and making them obedient to the truth. We can't question God's ability when He has clearly laid out a path of transformation. We must no longer feed thoughts that make us a playground for the enemy of our soul. We must take every thought captive that does not align to truth.

Additionally, I want you to pray every single day for the revelation of the love of God to fill you to fullness, releasing you from every symptom of the orphan spirit. The love of God brings with it acceptance, belonging, worthiness, and feeling chosen. It also brings a release from striving. There is power in both praying the Word aloud and meditating on the Word, so I encourage you to meditate on Ephesians 3:14-21, and then create a declaration that you are filled with the love of God and speak it aloud over your life.

_____

_____

_____

_____

_____

What symptoms do you have of the orphan spirit that you need to surrender to the Father? {Review list above.}

_____

_____

_____

_____

_____

_____

Prayer of Release of the Orphan Spirit

Father, I recognize that I may have agreed with a lie that has allowed the orphan spirit to deceive me from seeing the truth about who I am. I repent from all lies today that have bound me to feeling rejected, alone, or not belonging. I renounce every assignment on my life, because I came into agreement with these lies. I come out of agreement with these lies that I am alone, rejected, and don't belong. I ask Holy Spirit that you will speak truth to me now.

{Still yourself and listen to the Holy Spirit.}

_____
_____
_____
_____

I now replace these lies with Your truth:

{Decree His Truth}
**It is Your pleasure and will to call me
DAUGHTER!**
Ephesians 1:5-6

PRAYER

Father, I thank You that Your Word says that if *I believe in the name of Jesus and I receive Him, therefore I am a child of God.*[36]I declare today that I believe and receive Jesus as my Lord, and I am a child of the most high God. I thank You that You did not make us slaves, but gave us a spirit of adoption, and I receive a spirit of adoption today. I thank You for Your truth, and align myself to Your truth this day. I ask for a supernatural revelation of Your love that would draw me into a deeper understanding of being Your daughter.

In the name of Jesus,

Amen.

He speaks to my heart...

He wants you to know that the desires of your heart are valid. You long to be loved, chosen, and worthy, because it is part of your divine design. He set all of those desires into the depths of your heart![37]

_____

_____

_____

_____

_____

_____

_____

_____

_____

_____

_____

_____

_____

_____

_____

_____

_____

_____

_____

CHAPTER ELEVEN:

The Orphan Spirit - Part II

*I will not leave you as orphans;
I will come to you.*
John 14:18

I have found that most women are deeply entrenched in this spirit of not belonging. Not only does this spirit come against our inheritance as an heir, but it also will make us vulnerable to poor life choices. Many of us entangled in this spirit enter into relationships that are not designed for us, and they ultimately become unhealthy and even harmful. We simply believe we don't deserve better. We also may struggle with depression, oppression, or loneliness, believing that we are unlovable and unwanted. All of these symptoms are the attempt of Satan to keep us from the truth about our identity. Because this orphan spirit has such huge ramifications on a woman's life, and hinders us from stepping fully into our identity as the bride of Christ, I want us to dig a little deeper today.

The intent of this journal is not to free you in thirty days, but to guide you—at your pace — through the healing work that holds you captive outside of a life that God has for you. Freedom and healing are a part of your journey rather than your destination. As you walk in new levels of freedom, you will awaken to new levels of intimacy and identity—having removed the fortress erected in effort to self protect that instead kept a barrier from you aligning to truth. So I remind you to go at your own pace. If this is a struggle, do the work to uproot as much as you can. You need to dismantle every lie or vow that you have believed that would keep you attached to this orphan spirit.

TESTIMONY:

I recognized that I believed a lie that I was alone after seeing a glaring pattern in my life that led to exhaustion. I would do everything myself, and would rarely ask for help. I was worn out and weary and I wondered why no one could see how much I needed help and step up to help me. *How did those that professed they loved me not see how much I needed them?* This pattern ultimately led to the very people that I believe God sent into my life to help me eventually leaving me, because the closer they got to me, the stronger they felt the overriding belief of my heart bleeding out, 'I am alone.' Therefore, I ultimately rejected the very help I desperately needed. Now alone again, I would become bitter that no one could see my need, and no one cared enough to help me. The truth was that the walls I had erected around my heart, not only kept the heartache out, but they also kept the help out, too. This was a foundational lie for me that really impacted my life and destroyed many relationships. When I came out of agreement with this lie, I almost immediately saw people coming forth to help. With ease, I began to delegate things off of my plate, because the truth that I needed help was my truth now and the people closest to me were able to see my willingness to have their help.

Most of us don't realize the power of these core lies and vows that impact our entire lives. I had lived out this lie—I am alone—for so long, and it was embedded so deep in my soul that despite that I had a very present family, I was entrenched in the orphan spirit. Completely deceived, I wasted countless years feeling alone and rejected, damaged a number of relationships not allowing others close to me, and eventually ended up in a serious health crisis! I certainly didn't comprehend in the depths of my being the identity of a daughter who was chosen, welcomed, adored, protected, loved, and provided for, as the

Father so desires. I wonder if you, like me, have taken the bait of the enemy, and allowed the orphan spirit to sabotage the truth that you are His daughter?

ASSIGNMENT

In your quiet time, allow the Holy Spirit to guide you through any symptoms of the Orphan Spirit that you need to work through, such as the following:
{Circle the ones you need to pray through.}

Fear
Anxiety
Insecurity
Abandoned
Lonely
Rejection
Independence
Worried over Provision
Unprotected
Not Belonging
Performance Driven
Survival Mode
Uncovered
Getting Identity from Things or Works

Ask the Holy Spirit for an image of when each symptom was introduced into your life.

_____

_____

_____

Ask if you believed a lie, or made a vow or a judgement because of this situation He is revealing to you.

_____

_____

_____

_____

Ask Him His truth about what you believed.

_____

_____

_____

_____

Disconnect from the lie, vow, or judgement.
Recognize the Lie.
Repent for the Lie.
Renounce the Lie.
Receive His truth.
Replace the Lie with His truth.

Forgive anyone that may have caused you to believe the lie.

_____

_____

He speaks to my heart...

How great is the love the Father has lavished on us, that we should be called children of God! And that is what we are!
1 John 3:1

May you experience the love of God lavished upon you, His daughter, today!

_____

_____

_____

_____

_____

_____

_____

_____

_____

_____

_____

_____

_____

_____

_____

_____

_____

_____

CHAPTER TWELVE:

SOUL TIES

"Though your sins be like scarlet, they shall be white as snow."
Isaiah 1:18

My heart here is not to bring condemnation or shame, but rather to release you from both. To be released, you must first understand your soul and how you can be entangled in the depths of it. The Word of God says....

May God himself, the God of peace, sanctify you through and through. May your whole spirit, soul and body be kept blameless at the coming of our Lord Jesus Christ. 1 Thessalonians 5:23

Just as God is a trinity, you are a trinity with a spirit, soul, and body. For today, we will focus on your soul which encompasses your mind, will, and emotions. When you use the word heart for your metaphysical or emotional heart, you are speaking also to your soul.

So what is a SOUL TIE? Our SOUL, as we just stated, is our mind, will, and emotions. A TIE is something that binds, fastens, attaches, or restrains. Therefore, a SOUL TIE is an attachment in our mind, will, or emotions to a person or an object that can influence our choices and defines our identity. Much like a baby is attached to the mother in the womb via the umbilical cord, we can be spiritually attached to others. This attachment can influence our lives in a way that leads us to making decisions based on fear of man versus obedience to God. While sexual immorality may be obvious sin, fear of man—even our family—over God is also sin, and this truth we need to awaken to.

Soul ties are not all harmful. There are actually healthy and unhealthy soul ties. In the covenant marriage God creates a godly soul tie between man and woman.

"For this reason a man will leave his father and mother and be united to his wife, and they shall become one flesh."
Genesis 2:24

In scripture, we see that Ruth and Naomi were knit together, as were David and Jonathan:

And it came to pass, when he had made an end of speaking unto Saul, that the soul of Jonathan was knit with the soul of David, and Jonathan loved him as his own soul. 1 Samuel 18:1 KJV

Healthy relationships or soul ties bring us closer to God. Small groups can create healthy soul ties as they encourage one another to grow in Christ. An older woman mentoring a younger woman can create a healthy soul tie, as well. God designed us to have relationships, and encourages us to love one another. However, we can allow ungodly soul ties to form, and these ungodly ties are the ones we want to address today.

The word is clear that we are to flee from sexual immorality, but we live in a society that has deceived many to become immune to the destruction of sexual sin. Paul urges us to....

Flee from sexual immorality. All other sins a person commits are outside of the body, but whoever sins sexually, sins against their own body.
I Corinthians 6:18

Sexual sin—even from our past— affects our current relationships, our intimacy with our spouse, and our connecting with God. It also opens the door to the enemy of our souls to torment us with feelings of unworthiness. Even when these relationships end, spiritually we are still attached to the people of our past. Our souls have now been knit together. The enemy has done a great job of perverting what God deemed holy and desired to be beautiful. When we violate the will of God in this area of our lives, it usually results in shame or guilt that for some can become debilitating.

Or do you not know that the one who joins himself to a prostitute is one body with her? For He says, "THE TWO SHALL BECOME ONE FLESH."
1 Corinthians 6:16

Examples of Ungodly Soul Ties:

✦ Any person that you have been sexually active with outside of marriage is a soul tie.

✦ Anything that enthrones your heart more than God is a soul tie.

✦ Anything that separates intimacy between you and your husband can be a soul tie.

✦ A past emotional relationship that seems to interfere or hinder current relationships is a soul tie.

✦ A person that can make or break your day can be a soul tie.

✦ An adult that fears making decisions without her parents has a soul tie with the parents.

- A person that finds value / identity by the response to social media post can have a soul tie with social media.
- A person that would have anxiety over not having their cell phone can have an ungodly soul tie with the cell phone.
- Doing anything to hold on to a relationship to avoid the feeling of abandonment with a person is a sign of a soul tie.
- An extreme need for approval from someone is a sign of a soul tie.
- Problems with intimacy and boundaries can be signs of a soul tie.
- Lying and dishonesty can also be symptoms of a soul tie.

The truth is that there is a soul tie between you and every person you have been with sexually. So we need to be intentional to sever all of these relationships. Take a few moments and ask the Holy Spirit if there are relationships from your past from which you need to cut the cords, and hold tight to His truth:

But where sin increased, grace increased all the MORE. Romans 5:20

_____

_____

_____

We need to ask the Holy Spirit if there are emotional ties that are hindering us from living the full life with Jesus. Are there people in your life that you need their approval more than even God's approval? Are there people in your life that have the power to make or break your day? Are there people in your life that control your choices even as an adult?

_____

_____

_____

_____

_____

We need to ask the Holy Spirit if there are possessions or positions or statuses that are reigning in our hearts over the identity that we receive from God?

_____

_____

_____

_____

_____

What we do with our bodies is considered a form of worship. So today we will destroy the ties that have hindered our worship, and seek to get connected to the one who can transform us into His beautiful holy image.

Therefore, I urge you, brothers and sisters, in view of God's mercy, to offer your bodies as a living sacrifice, holy and pleasing to God--this is your true and proper worship.
Romans 12:1

But he who unites himself with the Lord is one with Him in spirit.
1 Corinthians 6:17

ACTIVATION:

With each area that the Holy Spirit showed you where soul ties are present, REPENT for sexual, emotional, or material attachment. RENOUNCE all attachments and sever all ties in Jesus name. Ask the Holy Spirit to speak to you if there are lies you believed that led to these attachments.

_____

_____

_____

If yes, renounce these lies and replace them with God's truth as we have done in the previous exercises.

Prayer to Break Soul Ties

With the power and authority of Jesus Christ, I break my bonding and connection with _____ and renounce any and all soul ties I have made because of these connections. I break off and cancel the effects these soul ties have had on my mind, my will, and my emotions. In the name of Jesus, I take back the ground of my soul where the enemy has sought to gain territory. I command the enemy to flee and never return. I am recommitting the ground of my soul to the Lordship of Jesus Christ. Jesus Christ is Lord of my Soul! Holy Spirit, I ask that you would purify and heal my broken heart. I ask that you would cleanse and renew my mind. With your power, realign my will to your will, empower me to make healthy, godly choices. Thank you for restoring and refreshing my emotions.

In Jesus name,

Amen

He speaks to my heart...

If there is shame or guilt because of your past, please know that He makes us clean.[38] Pour your heart out to Him today. Do not allow shame or guilt to reign in your heart while He offers freedom.

_____

_____

_____

_____

_____

_____

_____

_____

_____

_____

_____

_____

_____

_____

_____

_____

_____

_____

_____

_____

_____

CHAPTER THIRTEEN:

Mother And Father Wounds

Honor your Father and Mother (which is the first com-
mandment with a promise), so that it may be well with you,
and that you may live a long life on earth.
Ephesians 6:2-3

You need to understand that the enemy of your heart understands the justice system in heaven. I believe this is why the Word charges us to "Submit to God, resist the devil, and he will flee."[39]We are always either partnering with truth or partnering with the enemy. When we submit to God, the enemy must flee, but if we fall to his temptation then he has 'legal rights' to influence our lives, and even hinder our destiny.

"Settle matters quickly with your adver-
sary who is taking you to court. Do it while you
are still together on the way, or your adversary
may hand you over to the judge, and the judge
may hand you over to the officer, and you may be
thrown into prison." Matthew 5:25

We have many believers in prison by their own actions, because they don't understand the legal system of heaven. This is a topic I will explore deeper in later teachings, but for now, you need to understand that God is just, and we reap what we sow. The Word reveals God as the Righteous Judge[40] and scripture is full of legal language like witnesses, defender, testimonies, and courts. We need to understand that in God's divine nature of love He longs to bless us, but because He is JUST we ourselves hinder the blessings being released from the courts of Heaven by our words, actions, and choices.

I have learned that the enemy loves to use the Word of God to block the blessings of God's people. When we violate the Word of God, we open a door for the enemy to bring an assignment against us. If we haven't opened a door, the enemy has no right. Jesus took Satan's authority at the cross, so unless we give Satan access, he has none. I pray that through these teachings you are waking up to the power you possess and the freedom that is available.

It seems that most freedom ministry that I have done with people reveals a garden of weeds planted in early childhood. The enemy knows that none of us are perfect parents, and none of us have perfect parents. He will tempt us to make vows or speak judgements against our parents, so that we dishonor them in a season of our lives when we really don't understand or can even comprehend the ramifications of such vows and judgements. If we dishonor the word of God that calls us to honor our parents, we open a door giving the enemy access to our lives that may ultimately turn to torment, and will most likely be replicated in our children, because the Word says,

"Do not be deceived: God cannot be mocked. A man reaps what he sows."
Galatians 6:7

This is also a very good reason why we, as parents, can't tolerate disrespect or feel guilty when we hold our children accountable to honor and respect us. We are raising a very rebellious generation, and many parents have lost their roles as parents, believing they are to be 'friends' rather than parents to their children. We are dangerously deceived if we think we are doing them good by allowing them to continue in such rebellion, because we are in essence giving the enemy access to our children. The rebellion today has opened children up in ways former generations would have never conceived.

I want you to know that I understand that some of you have experienced great tragedy by the hands, words, and actions of parents. Some of you have been neglected and rejected by those that should have loved, affirmed, and protected you. Some of you have even been physically violated. The depths of the pain for some of you is overwhelming, and for others is so deeply hidden that you may deny it exists. The truth is that there is fruit of our pain no matter how deep you have suppressed it. There is fruit of our dishonor no matter how deserving your parents may be of it. If we truly want to be free, we must realize that we have one enemy.

We wrestle not with flesh, but with principalities[41], and these principalities know those that would hurt us most: parents, siblings, close friends, and spouses. In effort to cause us to open doors so that he may have access to our hearts, Satan influences those that would hurt us most as tools to wound us deeply. Wounded, we will make vows or judgements or dishonor our parents, which violates the Word of God and gives the enemy access to our lives. As we discussed earlier, Satan is desperate to silence us, and since it is out of the abundance of our heart that we *speak*,[42] he pokes most where it hurts our hearts the deepest.

We need to walk through closing some doors today, in effort to find our voices. I know this can be tough and tearful, so I commend you for being willing!

Can you accept that some people that have hurt you deeply, truly have no idea the depth of your pain? I would venture to say that those that have hurt you don't remember the details that you can't seem to forget.

Could you model the life of Jesus today, and choose to forgive and release those that you have held captive to your pain?

Could you choose to take it a step further and bless your family?

Could you be the voice of redemption that will bring your family into the Kingdom of God on Earth?

Are you willing to take God at His Word and trust Him?

I pray you are saying, "Yes!"

TESTIMONY:

I led a woman, we will call Lacey, through freedom ministry seeking to heal her relationship with her teenage daughter, Amy, and her husband. Her story is a great example of how seeds of judgement in your childhood can almost sabotage your life. It seemed that despite how much Lacey sought to show love and support to Amy, her daughter remained very distant, and despite how much her husband professed his love for her, she felt unworthy and unloved. I began as I usually do, asking questions about Lacey's relationship with her own parents. As I expected, she said something like, "I keep my distance, because our relationship is a little toxic." I knew right away we were looking at childhood judgements, so instead of focusing in on Amy or her husband, I dug deep into the childhood of Lacey.

As Lacey begins to share her childhood, the vows and judgements raise their heads quickly. Her childhood home was loud from her parents constant confrontation and dysfunction. Her parents, both wounded from their own childhood, never sought counseling, or God, and certainly not freedom ministry, but rather replicated what they knew as "normal." As a young girl, Lacey believed that her parent's relationship was toxic. Add to the toxicity between her parents, her relationship with her parents she believed was toxic, too. She began to distance herself from the toxicity. She then watched as the friendships of her parents edified this belief that relationships are toxic, because all the women seemed to do was gossip, drink excessively, degrade other women, and eventually betray one another. She now believed that all relationships are toxic. To add to all of this toxicity, she believed that her mother was weak for staying in all of these relationships, so she judged her mother as weak, and vowed she would never be so weak to stay in such a toxic marriage or toxic friendships.

Now fast forward to her adult life, and Lacey has experienced too many broken relationships to count. She has been married multiple times, because the moment she feels weak she jumps ship. She doesn't let women get close to her, because she has experienced too much betrayal and "toxicity" with women. Lacey is now struggling with her relationship with her own daughter who is "keeping her distance," despite Lacey's efforts to raise her daughter in a healthy atmosphere. Are you seeing the patterns?

Lacey began the freedom process to try to understand her relationship with her daughter, heal her relationship with her parents, and to open the pathway to healthier relationships with both her husband and women going forward. Knowing that most current relationships can be reflections of our early childhood relationships, we decided to ask the Father what she truly believed about her parents. In exploring her child-hood roots, we could dismantle the vows and judgements that had made her a target to reap a lifestyle of dysfunction despite her efforts to avoid such dysfunction.

As we surrendered to the Holy Spirit, we found she had many beliefs that led to judgements or vows against her parents:

Beliefs /Judgement	Vow
They weren't good parents.	She would never be like her parents.
They didn't protect her.	She would self protect.
Their relationships were toxic.	All relationships are toxic.
They didn't love her.	I am unloved.
My mother is weak.	I will never be weak.
My father is ungodly.	I will never marry someone like him.

Recognizing that we had several judge-ments, we also could see that the judgements had led her to reap what she had sown against them and herself. She had toxic relationships, attracted ungodly men just like her father, and though she left at the first sign of weakness, she ultimately felt helpless and completely unworthy of a life that looked different from what had become her "normal."

The good news is that in recognizing the patterns that had come from the seeds of judgment in her childhood, we were able to disarm them from affecting her life any longer. She repented for each lie and judgement, she forgave her parents, and she even blessed them for being her source of life. She also forgave the men and women in her life that had edified the lie that relationships are toxic.

Within the month, Lacey reported that the tension in her relationships had left. Her relationship with her daughter and her mother shifted and had grown closer. Women began to pursue her for friendship, she was actually experiencing a deeper intimacy with her husband, and she was finally able to receive his love for her. As the walls of judgement came down, the blessings of God were able to pour in.

I share this testimony with you, because often we don't realize that we have these deeper underlying beliefs that are bearing some undesirable fruit in our lives. Many times we accept dysfunctional and fruitless lifestyles as normal, when God calls us to flourish.

ACTIVATION:

Ask the Holy Spirit to show you a MEMORY of
an event/events that may have caused you to
make vows or judgements against your parents.
{Look for memories that hold keys to vows.}

Ask the Holy Spirit if you believed a lie as a
result of this event.

Then, ask if you made vows or judgements as a
result of the lie or lies.
{This could take hours or days, so be willing to sit.}

Lie I Believed   Vow or Judgment

_____

_____

_____

_____

_____

_____

_____

_____

_____

Now take each one of these and follow our protocol:
Recognize the Lie.
Repent for the Lie.
Renounce the Lie.
Receive His truth.
Replace the Lie with His truth.

He speaks to my heart...

Now, we want to reverse the curse by blessing your earthly source of life. Can you speak life over your mother and father?

_____

_____

_____

_____

_____

_____

_____

_____

_____

_____

_____

_____

_____

_____

_____

_____

_____

_____

_____

_____

SECTION THREE:

Freeing
Captives

CHAPTER FOURTEEN:

STRONGHOLDS

*For though we walk in flesh, we do not war according to flesh. For the weapons of our warfare are not carnal, but mighty through God to the pulling down of **strong holds**; Casting down imaginations, and every high thing that exalts itself against the knowledge of God, and bringing into captivity every thought to the obedience of Christ;*
2 Corinthians 10:4-5

Strongholds are thoughts that exalt themselves above the truth of God. These thoughts may seem innocent, but when they become beliefs, they can be the driving force of our lives. They ultimately have a *strong* hold on us.

There is often a pattern to forming a stronghold. This usually begins in one of three ways:

1.) A traumatic experience usually in early childhood.
2.) The absence of what is needed as a child such as protection, nurturing, love, and affirmation.
3.) Generational iniquity.

As a result of one of these events, our response is to believe a lie. In effort to protect ourselves from ever experiencing this pain or trauma again, we then begin to erect coping mechanisms. Remember that the enemy of our heart is the father of lies. All lies originate from the enemy of our heart, and when we choose to believe these lies, it is much like partnering with the enemy and granting him access to play with our head.

What ultimately happens is that we believe that by erecting these coping mechanisms—sarcasm, blame, denial, isolation, etc—we protect ourselves from ever being weak, exposed, and vulnerable again, but inevitably, we partner with the enemy and become a target to the very thing we seek to prevent. Many of us can hide our pain well, until we are in relationships, but relationships have a way of exposing what lies beneath. Most often, someone we are close to will poke the wound which triggers the emotions attached to that original event, and in effort to self-protect, we react in a way that often perpetuates the event all over again.

For example: An event happens to you as a child with a man be it your father, grandfather, brother, uncle, or a stranger. The enemy tempts you to believe a lie that all men will hurt you. Because you believe this lie that all men will hurt you, you vow, "I will never trust men." Now you will use a coping mechanism to protect your heart from men. You may use sarcasm, self-sabotage, isolation, or humor to keep men from getting close to you. When a man does get close to you, your walls push him away and now you have set him up to build on this lie that men can't be trusted, because like the others he, too, leaves you. Even unknowingly you can be reliving a childhood wound.

Another common lie: You were neglected as a child because your family worked long days and late hours. You began to take care of your own needs, even as a child. The enemy tempts you with the lie that you are alone. This lie becomes a vow, 'I am alone.' Your coping mechanism becomes busyness and performance to meet your own needs. You don't let people in to help you, because you believe you are alone and no one cares. You hinder healthy relationships, because you become controlling and demanding, believing if you don't do it, then no one will. This then leads to bitterness, because you resent people for not helping you carry the weight. Since those that you love aren't helping you bear your load, you now feel alone once again. The problem is what seemed to be a little lie has actually become a stronghold that comes against the word of God which says, "I will never leave or forsake you." This lie 'I am alone' sets you up to strive, control, blame, and become bitter. Now what seemed noble and caused you to take on the world alone, has contributed to the toxicity of your soul and created a life that bears the fruit of your lips—alone!

Lies that become deep rooted beliefs now impact our daily life much more than we realize. These lies begin to have a hold on us.

Be careful how you think, your life is shaped by your thoughts.
Proverbs 4:23

I think I annoy my husband because I have done so much freedom ministry, it seems I have a freedom radar. I will look at him and say, "Baby, you know that's a vow right?" as he buys every single item at the concession stand at our high school football game! He then tucks his popcorn, nachos, peanuts, candy bar and sprite under his arm and walks away with the guilt of a two year old little boy all over his face. I have never seen anyone buy as much junk food at a football game as my husband. I personally could avoid it all, but he is like a kid in a candy store. I am not sure what the vow is exactly because he won't say anything more than I'm right, but I would bet it was something like this: he didn't have any money to buy snacks at the ball field when he was younger, so he vowed that he would buy whatever he wanted as an adult. And he does just that!

This vow hasn't caused detrimental harm to our family and it may not be a stronghold, but it certainly reveals there is something layered deeper in his heart. And though it seems insignificant, there could be a fear of trusting God ultimately underlying it, because of a childhood season of going without. If this root is not tended to, it will eventually show itself to his detriment or his waistline. I haven't found men to be as open to this digging up of roots as women are, but I will say that the work my husband and I have done together has truly transformed our marriage.

For now, your focus is to simply work on the woman in the mirror. These examples are here to hopefully poke some places in your heart where you, too, may have believed a lie that comes against the word of God. I believe as the men in our lives see how differently we live and speak and carry ourselves as a result of this season, that they too will desire truth in their hearts, and with truth comes freedom!

Common strongholds in women:

I am alone.

My life will never get easier.

I am not enough.

I can't be weak.

I can't trust people not to betray.

It is up to me to provide.

Men are _____.

Fear of man over God.

No Godly man would love me.

I have to work harder than others to be seen.

I must protect myself.

Never depend on others.

Relationships are toxic.

I could never _____.

Common Generational or cultural strongholds:

Italians are hot tempered.

Texans are_____.

Southerners are _____.

Methodist are private with our faith.

God is disappointed in us.

These are all lies that can become beliefs based off of life experiences, our family, or culture.

Today, ask the Father to show you a lie you may have believed that has become a stronghold in your life.

_____

_____

_____

_____

Look for a memory.

_____

_____

_____

Ask what lie you believed because of this event?

_____

_____

_____

_____

Did you make a vow?

_____

_____

_____

Now we want to invite Jesus into this memory. Ask Jesus where He was when this event happened and what would He like to say to you about this event? We need His truth to override the lies you have allowed to grow.

_____

_____

_____

_____

_____

It is important that we take difficult memories and invite Jesus in to heal those memories. Sometimes we have to go back just one more time to grab hold of our healing. Can you see Jesus comforting you in the memory? Try to imagine Him there with you, reassuring you and speaking truth to uproot these lies and vows.

Now dismantle the lie or vow or both:

Recognize the Lie.
Repent for the Lie.
Renounce the Lie.
Receive His truth.
Replace the Lie with His truth.

Now when the enemy seeks to get you to come into agreement with that lie again, you will speak to Him the truth you received just as Jesus did...

It is written that _____

{God never leaves or forsakes me. I am a royal priesthood and a holy nation and completely worthy.}

He speaks to my heart...

The Lord is my rock, my fortress and my deliverer; my God is my rock, in whom I take refuge, my shield and the horn of my salvation, my STRONGHOLD.
Psalm 18:2

_____

_____

_____

_____

_____

_____

_____

_____

_____

_____

_____

_____

_____

_____

_____

_____

CHAPTER FIFTEEN:

STRONGHOLDS II

Where the Spirit of the Lord is there is
FREEDOM!
2 Corinthians 3:17

We enter another day of inviting the Spirit of the Lord into the recesses of our hearts to re-wire these deeply embedded vows that have held us captive or become strongholds. These lies, while seemingly innocent, hinder us from living out the life of fullness Jesus offers. Since we are seeking true freedom, we will surrender to a little more open heart surgery today!

I found, in my own heart, that there were *many* strongholds buried deep, so take as many days as you need to sit at His feet and dig deeper. Many of us have generational strongholds, which we will discuss further in the next chapter, or patterns that are so familiar to our families that we don't realize we can exist without them. Some of us are even deceived to think that our behavior, because it is so familiar, may even be godly when in fact it may not be at all. This lie that 'it has always been this way, so it will always be this way,' has entrenched families all the way back to the Garden of Eden. God is always looking for someone to break off generational bondage, and we will talk about this topic in more detail later, but for now we will look at beliefs that have been passed down in our families, and how we can dismantle them. The first step is always to recognize that it is an area we need to invite the spirit in to heal us or free us from.

Since we have launched our church, The Well, freedom ministry has been part of our church DNA. We believe God has called us to lead families to freedom, and we know that free people free people, so to take a city for the Kingdom of God we need an army of free people, right? On this journey with our church family, it has been wonderful to watch families restored and lives redeemed as our people awaken to the strategies of the enemy to steal their peace or finances or relationships, and they take back their authority. We have even begun to introduce exercises in our children's ministry to help our children hopefully prevent some of the patterns we have all lived to our detriment. One family that I have watched really pursue freedom has a great example of a generational stronghold that I believe will show you the impact of generational strongholds.

TESTIMONY

Their home is the home that is always full of children. They are the house where people gather for meals, for fellowship, and to celebrate. Their policy is always an open door. The love of family is evident by those looking in, and the feeling of acceptance exudes this place. However, the teenage daughter is struggling with rejection. In doing freedom ministry, she seeks to find the root of this rejection. Her life does not speak rejection, yet her heart is experiencing it.

Through her ministry time, she uncovers that some of her rejection comes from her father, because he works long hours, and misses some events. She is longing for more of his attention. Of course, this news is shocking to the father who only works long hours to meet the needs of his family, and in his mind this is what love is—working hard to provide. When he was a young man, his father worked hard to provide. It was how he showed love, so as a young boy, this man makes a vow, even unknowingly, that working hard makes him a good father. Obviously, working hard is a great attribute of a father who sees his role as providing, but this role of providing doesn't override the families need for his presence. Do you see in this scenario how the heart of the father was to show love, but the daughter didn't see it? In finding the root of rejection, she was able to identify a generational stronghold on men in their family that said, 'To show love you work hard and provide.' This belief coupled with the responsibility on men to provide can dangerously position men to lean not on God, but their own hands for provision. The answer when we recognize a pattern like this is repentance. We must seek to renew our thought pattern and start moving in an opposite direction.

My heart in sharing stories like this with you is to awaken you to your own story. Perhaps you too have felt rejected by a father believing that you aren't worthy of his time, because he is held by a lie that a good father shows love by provision. Don't get me wrong, it is great that our fathers provide, but we also need their protection, affirmation, and their presence. How we see our earthly father can impact our relationship with our heavenly father, thus the enemy works hard to sabotage this relationship. The truth about this story above is that the father dearly loves his daughter, and it breaks his heart that she has felt even one moment of rejection. It is imperative that we seek truth instead of believing the enemy's lie.

As we learned yesterday, there is usually a pattern to the forming of a stronghold. In this pattern, we react with a defense mechanism to avoid pain or trauma that we have experienced in the past. Today, I want you to look at this list of defense mechanisms and see if you recognize any of these in your life, because it could be a key that a stronghold is hidden behind the defense mechanism.

Common Defense/Coping Mechanisms:

Anger

Blame

Busyness

Control

Denial

Isolation

Over Reasoning

Paranoid

People Pleasing

Refusing to Trust

Self Sabotage

Sarcasm

Are any of these coping mechanisms familiar to you? The Word tells us to guard our hearts, but instead of healthy guarding, many of us have erected a fortress around our hearts. Ask the Father where this coping mechanism entered into your life?

_____

_____

_____

_____

I realize, Father, that I am using _____
as a coping mechanism. I know _____
is not a fruit of Your Spirit and comes against Your truth. I ask you to show me where I opened the door to _____.

Look for a memory.

_____

_____

_____

_____

Did I believe a lie in this moment?

_____

_____

_____

_____

Did I make a vow based off of this lie that has become a stronghold?

_____

_____

_____

_____

_____

Father, what is Your Truth about this lie/vow?

_____

_____

_____

Now follow our protocol or as you are led by the Spirit:

Recognize the Lie.
Repent for the Lie.
Renounce the Lie.
Receive His truth.
Replace the Lie with His truth.

We are learning a process that will help you as you continue on this journey to freedom. You may not be aware, but it takes seven times to refine silver, and much like silver we are being refined to the value God intended. This could be painful or take much longer than you desire. However the outcome is worth it! You are worth the work to step into what is fully available.

He speaks to my heart...

Spend some time thinking about your life. What do you love? Where do you wish you flourished more? What do you dread? What would you change? Is it possible that you have believed a lie that has become a stronghold that has you stagnant instead of flourishing?

_____

_____

_____

_____

_____

_____

_____

_____

_____

_____

_____

_____

_____

_____

_____

_____

_____

_____

_____

CHAPTER SIXTEEN:

GENERATIONAL BONDAGE

"You shall not worship them or serve them; for I, the LORD your God, am a jealous God, visiting the iniquity of the fathers on the children, on the third and the fourth generations of those who hate Me, but showing lovingkindness to thousands, to those who love Me and keep My commandments. Exodus 20:5-6

The idea was that God would use family to pass down through generations the blessings of God, but the reality is that lies, dysfunction, and sickness have held families captive for generations instead. Some of our family patterns are so familiar, we are deceived from seeing that they are far from the intentions of God. This is why the first step is always recognizing. If we can just see that what we are struggling with doesn't have to remain, then we can do something about the areas that are plaguing our families. If we are blinded to the truth that we have a problem, it will be impossible to break free from it.

Gateway church, in my opinion, seems to have the best definition of a generational iniquity:

An unholy spiritual influence, an open door or tendency in a family's lineage, or an acceptance of something that controls the behavior of many in a family and is viewed as "normal."

There are some things in your family that seem normal yet cause you to almost feel like you are losing your ever loving mind. There are some things in your family that you said you would never do, yet you find yourself doing or saying them. There are some things in your family that have caused you to avoid family reunions. I have wonderful news for you that these struggles don't have to continue forward in your family. God is looking for someone to stand in the blood line of the family and repent on behalf of the family and reclaim the family's inheritance. Don't worry, you are not alone. Generational bondage has been a part of our history all the way back to Abraham.

Here are just a few patterns in scripture of generational bondage. We see favoritism passed down from Abraham with his son Isaac. Then, Isaac's wife, Rebekah, favors their son Jacob over Esau, and she plots with Jacob to steal the blessing of the first born from Esau. Then, Jacob favors his wife Rachel over Leah. He also favors Rachel's first born son, Joseph, over his other sons. The favoritism is passed on from generation to generation. With the favoritism also came lying, deceit, division, and conflict, as we saw Jacob deceive his father, so that he would get the blessing of Esau. We saw the father of Rachel deceive Jacob, and give him Leah as his wife instead of Rachel. We later see the children of Jacob deceive their father that Joseph was dead, so they would no longer compete for his affection, and ultimately Joseph deceived his brothers to his true identity as a leader in Egypt.

Many today would argue that we aren't under the curse of the law, which is true, but ministry would tell you that people today are bound by iniquity that touches generations.

Christ has redeemed us from the curse of the law, having become a curse for us, that the blessing of Abraham might come upon the Gentiles in Christ Jesus, that we might receive the promise of the Spirit through faith.
Galatians 3:13-14

God redeemed us from the curse through Jesus that we might have the blessings of Abraham come upon us. My experience is that the blessings of Abraham are available, but we need to be intentional about recognizing open doors in our family lineage and closing them, so that the blessings of Abraham are upon us rather than the dysfunction or disease of our families.

Look at the list below and see if you see patterns of these items displayed in multiple family members.

Generational Iniquity List:

- Abuse (emotional, physical, mental, sexual)
- Addictions
- Anger, rage, violence
- Control and manipulation
- Critical Spirit, Jealousy
- Disability and Entitlement
- Emotional dependency
- Fears and Anxiety
- Financial patterns of losing money
- Hatred for Women or Men or Race
- Idolatry
- Laziness, Poverty
- Lying
- Mental Illness
- Murder, Suicide, Accidents, Early Death
- Not caring for children
- Parents/Children exchanging roles
- Physical deformities

- Pride and rebellion
- Rejection and insecurity
- Religious bondage and cults
- Occult or secret organizations
- Sexual sin
- Unbelief
- Unworthiness and low self-esteem
- Victimization

The good news is that every one of these iniquities is redeemable through Jesus Christ.

All of us like sheep have gone astray, Each of us has turned to his own way; But the LORD has caused the iniquity of us all to fall on Him.
Isaiah 53:6

It is clear in scripture that we are to confess generational iniquity and break it off :

The LORD is slow to anger and abundant in lovingkindness, forgiving iniquity and transgression; but He will by no means clear the guilty, visiting the iniquity of the fathers on the children to the third and the fourth generations.
Numbers 14:18 (NASB)

If they confess their iniquity and the iniquity of their forefathers, in their unfaithfulness which they committed against Me, and also in their acting with hostility against Me. I also was acting with hostility against them, to bring them into the land of their enemies—or if their uncircumcised heart becomes humbled so that they then make amends for their iniquity, then I will remember My covenant with Jacob, and I will remember also My covenant with Isaac, and My covenant with Abraham as well, and I will remember the land.
Leviticus 26:40-42 (NASB)

You may need to spend several days on this list of generational iniquity, because it is important that you plead the blood of Jesus over every area of generational bondage.

PRAYER

I thank You, Father, that Your perfect son, Jesus, took on every iniquity that has plagued my family for generations. I stand in the gap today pleading the blood of Jesus over my family line all the way back to Adam. I stand in the gap today for the _____ family to release the blessings of God over my family. Lord, I repent on behalf of the _____ family for giving place to _____ {Name Iniquity}. I receive Your forgiveness on behalf of our entire family. By the authority of Jesus Christ, I renounce any and all works of darkness associated with _____{Name Iniquity.} I close every door opened due to _____ {Name Iniquity], and I break the power that has kept my family imprisoned to this iniquity. I confess that Jesus Christ is the Lord of our family. I thank You that because we believe in You, we are called Your children. I thank You that the blessings of the Father are upon us, and will go forward thousands of generations according to Your Word. Thank you today that the work of Jesus is complete and sealed, and the blood of Jesus covers us all.

In Jesus Name,
Amen.

He speaks to my heart...

What does it mean to you that you are a child of God carrying DIVINE DNA? As a child of God, what is your inheritance? Ask Him.

_____

_____

_____

_____

_____

_____

_____

_____

_____

_____

_____

_____

_____

_____

_____

_____

_____

_____

_____

_____

CHAPTER SEVENTEEN:

RELEASING JUDGEMENTS

"Do not judge, or you too will be judged. For in the same way you judge others, you will be judged, and with the measure you use, it will be measured to you."
Matthew 7:1-2

The Word is clear that we aren't to judge. It even says that as we judge, we are judged. So if you can imagine that every time you speak {*Life and death are in your tongue*—Proverbs 18:21} you have an imaginary bullseye that comes right up on your head, and whatever you speak ultimately comes back to you. You have vowed that men are crazy, so you now have a target on your head for crazy men. You are basically a magnet to them. Vows and judgements often go hand in hand, because typically a vow is made because of a judgement.

Have you ever said something like…

I will never marry someone like my father and then you realize you did?

Or perhaps…

I will never be like my mother and yet you are?

Or even…

All men are crazy and then you can't escape crazy men?

Or how about…

My life will never be as easy as hers and it never is?

As you are hearing these different scenarios, I can imagine you are having flash backs and perhaps covering your lips. Oooops! We have all done it. We have all thrown around judgments with absolutely zero malice in our heart, yet our lives are bearing fruit of the words carelessly spoken that come against what God says about us and others.

Could you be reaping seeds of your own vows or judgements? An easy way to identify if you are reaping such seeds is to look at the patterns that are shaping your life. Patterns are keys to the seeds sown from vows and judgments. I realize that this process can be difficult to digest, but I want you to shift from condemnation or regret as you see the patterns that have followed your life, to thankfulness that you have arrived at this place where you can handle God showing you these patterns. As we are ready, the Holy Spirit can show us the places in our hearts that He is ready to release or heal.

After this exercise, I pray that you will begin to notice other patterns that have hindered your inheritance and begin to seek revelation to their roots quickly. So let's take some time today to explore such patterns.

Sit quietly asking the Father to reveal to you any of these patterns that could be impacting your life. Circle each pattern that resonates with your history.

Do you have a pattern of distrust?

Do you have a pattern of losing finances?

Do you have a pattern of no one helping you?

Do you have a pattern of being overlooked?

Do you have a pattern of busyness?

Do you have a pattern of men that don't help you financially?

Do you have a pattern of abuse or betrayal?

Do you have a pattern of men presenting themselves as one way and actually being something different? {Aka: Fraud}

Do you have a pattern of being falsely accused?

Do you feel the need to control?

Do you blame?

Do people question your motives?

Do you seem to be critical of others?

Do women that get close to you betray you?

Do people come into your life to help, but they always leave?

Patterns are signs that vows and judgements are most likely present. You will need to take each pattern and look at them individually, asking the Holy Spirit to show you if there is a judgement or a vow that has led to this pattern. Here is a common example:

The pattern is that men come into your life acting like prince charming, yet they always end up taking your breath and your freedom as their charm turns to control. You feel distrusting, deceived, and betrayed. You believe that all men are the same, and none can be trusted. If you explored deeper the root of this pattern, you may find something like this: The seed of judgement came as a child watching your father control and emotionally abuse your mother. As a result of his abuse, you judged him as being angry, controlling, and not a good father. Then you vowed that men are controlling and you would never marry a man like your father. However, you are now living out the very thing you said you never would. In essence, this is how judgements influence our lives.

The key to dismantling the judgement or vow is repenting. Repenting and confession are two different things. Confession says we are wrong, but repentance chooses to walk away from belief or action or thought. If you feel something like this…"I forgive him, but I still want to kill him!" then you are confessing, not repenting. Repentance is a desire to have heart change. If you recognize that you have a need to repent, but you honestly aren't capable of repenting, then confess the vow or judgement and ask the Holy Spirit to lead you to repentance. *The kindness of God leads us to repentance.*[43]

Judgements often happen much like this scenario above when we are younger and are easy prey to an enemy that seeks to devour us. These judgements are often against our parents, because if the enemy can get us to make judgements against our parents, he has us violating the Word of God in two areas: Judgements and Honoring our Mother and Father. His hope is that he can tempt us into violating the Word of God, so that he has rights to interfere with our lives. If you submit to God's truth and resist him, he has no rights. As we are repenting, we are taking back our rights and dismissing him and his assignments from our life.

ASSIGNMENT

Take every pattern that you recognized today, and bring it to the Holy Spirit. I recognize that I have a pattern of _____. Holy Spirit will you show me if I sowed a seed of judgement that has led me to reaping this pattern?

If you have a pattern that is obvious, but was not listed above, please bring it to Jesus today too.

Pattern 1:_____

The Holy Spirit showed me: _____

_____

_____

_____

_____

_____

Recognize the judgement.
Repent from the judgement.
Renounce the pattern over your life.
Receive God's truth.
Replace the judgement with God's truth.

Pattern 2:_____

The Holy Spirit showed me: _____

_____

_____

_____

_____

_____

Recognize the judgement.
Repent from the judgement.
Renounce the pattern over your life.
Receive God's truth.
Replace the judgement with God's truth.

Pattern 3:_____
The Holy Spirit showed me: _____

_____
_____
_____
_____
_____

Recognize the judgement.
Repent from the judgement.
Renounce the pattern over your life.
Receive God's truth.
Replace the judgement with God's truth.

Pattern 4:_____
The Holy Spirit showed me: _____

_____
_____
_____
_____
_____

Recognize the judgement.
Repent from the judgement.
Renounce the pattern over your life.
Receive God's truth.
Replace the judgement with God's truth.

He speaks to my heart...

I believe the Father wants you to know that He understands....What would you say back to Him today?

_____

_____

_____

_____

_____

_____

_____

_____

_____

_____

_____

_____

_____

_____

_____

_____

_____

_____

_____

_____

_____

_____

CHAPTER EIGHTEEN:

JUDGEMENTS THAT HINDER DIVINE ASSIGNMENTS

Create in me a pure heart, O God,
and renew a steadfast spirit within me.
Do not cast me from your presence or take Your Holy Spirit
from me. Restore to me the joy of your salvation
and grant me a willing spirit, to sustain me.
Psalm 51:10-12

Do you desire a pure heart before the Lord? I know there were many seasons of my life when I thought my heart was pure, but I would eventually find out that hidden deep inside were dark places that I didn't even realize were a part of my heart. Our hearts are like beautiful diamonds, where sometimes the flaws are glaringly obvious, and yet other times they are so hidden it takes special tools to even find the dark recesses. Today, we will look again at judgements, but specifically we will look at judgements that may have impacted or hindered our destiny, and may be deeply hidden in the places of our heart that we are unaware of.

TESTIMONY

There was a season where it felt like people that I loved dearly and had invested much in to their spiritual growth would question the purity of my heart. It made no sense that those I longed to lift up with great sincerity of heart questioned my intentions. I will admit that I was grieving the loss of relationships, and questioning God for the answer because to me it made no sense. Seeing my broken spirit, my husband even defended me to one person, saying, "I have never met a woman with a more pure heart than my wife."

I had recently spent some time looking at patterns, and I began to see that this was becoming a pattern, too. I humbled myself, and asked the Holy Spirit to show me if I was reaping a seed of judgement that had led those I cared deeply about to miss my heart to help them. Almost instantly, I had a memory of a time that I had attended a women's conference. One of the speakers did not sit well with my spirit. To be transparent, I judged her as being a marketing genius rather than having a pure heart as a Bible teacher. I didn't buy her books, and I never again attended an event that she was involved in because I believed she was marketing rather than serving Jesus. In the moment of this judgement, I believed I was 'guarding my heart' from someone that had impure motives, but in reality I was making judgements against someone that I knew very little about. I was grieved at this new awareness of how dishonoring I had been to someone who was living out the destiny that I felt called to, also. Ultimately, my heart had not been pure in judging her, which grieved me even more.

Realizing that I had sown this seed of judgement against a pure heart, I dismantled the judgement by repenting and pleading the blood of Jesus over my words, actions, and thoughts. Within days of this repentance, those relationships were restored. I will say that this was a moment where it was necessary for my tears of repentance to flow. I believe that our Father longs for us to get to a place where we are broken over the condition of our hearts, and in our brokenness, he meets us there.

The Lord is close to the brokenhearted
and saves those who are crushed in spirit.
Psalm 34:18

I believe this judgement not only attracted me to reap the same judgement against my heart, but it influenced the perception of me as a Bible teacher, as well. Have you made judgments against people that are living out the life you long for? This may be different for all of us. If you long to be a mother, and have found yourself criticizing others who are mothers, you need to cleanse your heart of this thought. If you are a single woman longing to be married, and have said things like, "How has she gotten a husband and not me," then you need to cleanse your heart. If you have longed to be a writer and have a book published, but you criticize other's writing because you know you could do better…cleanse. If you are in financial devastation, but you have continuously criticized how other people have used their money, you need to cleanse. If you have criticized someone's parenting skills and now you are living with destructive, adult children running your life, perhaps you need to cleanse your heart?

The pure in heart will see Him.
Matthew 5:8

When we truly desire to get closer to Him —to see Him—we are willing to do the work of uprooting the truth about what lies beneath the surface. To live from a pure heart that is rooted in love, we must detox and uproot the current system. As we have done the past few days, when you realize there is a judgement, recognize the judgement and name it, repent from speaking the judgement, renounce the assignments on your life due to the judgement, replace the judgement with truth and receive wisdom from the Holy Spirit. At this point, I would suggest you speak blessings and life over the person that you have judged to further reverse the judgement.

He speaks to my heart...

Father, show us today the thoughts and motives of our hearts that aren't pure and holy. Create in us a clean heart. Renew in us a steadfast spirit. Psalm 51:10 May You pour out Your blessings upon our lives.

_____

_____

_____

_____

_____

_____

_____

_____

_____

_____

_____

CHAPTER NINETEEN:

RELEASING ANGER

We must never rest until everything
inside of us worships God.
A. W. Tozer

This is an area that most women would
deny they struggle with, yet we all have come to
a place, either gradually or abruptly, that we find
ourselves face to face with an explosion. It is almost automatic that we begin to look outward,
certain that someone else is responsible for our
behavior. What I have learned is that anger is to
our soul what pain is to our body. When we have
continuous physical pain, we know that it is time
to consult a physician. When we have continual
emotional eruptions, we should be alerted to
check in with not just any physician, but the
Great Physician. Anger is basically a fire alarm
alerting us that something isn't right, or that
something is seriously wrong.

Andy Stanley has a great video from his
"Staying In Love" series featuring Mr. and Mrs.
Mug. The Mugs are represented by a mug full of
pink beads and a mug full of blue beads. Andy
intentionally bumps Mr. & Mrs. Mug together,

demonstrating how pink comes out of Mrs. Mug and blue comes out of Mr. Mug every time they collide. At no time in this friction does pink come out of Mr. Mug or blue come out of Mrs. Mug. Though we want to blame the blue man for causing our pink stuff to come out, the Word of God is clear that out of the abundance of the heart our mouths speak[44]. What is inside of us, inevitably will come out!

I love how A.W. Tozer says that we must never rest until everything inside of us is worshipping God. As long as we are pointing out and casting blame on others, we will never look deeper inward to find the healing that is available. Trying to control your anger may seem noble and certainly healthy for those in your family, but it will never lead to lasting freedom. We must desire truth in our innermost being, and then pursue that truth, asking the harder question: What is *my* part in this response of anger?

Like everything else we have ventured to discuss thus far, anger has underlying roots. Anger is typically a secondary emotion, not a primary emotion, which is why it is vital that we go deeper to explore the roots of anger. Anger is usually secondary to:

• Hurt
• Fear

- Shame
- Inferiority
- Rejection
- Grief {Anger is one of the five steps of the grieving process.}

Most of us associate anger with explosive responses, but truthfully anger encompasses much more than a temper. The symptoms of anger include:

- Irritation, Agitation, and Frustration
- Sarcasm
- Cold Shoulder or Silent Treatment
- Fury or Rage
- Fleeing from conflict
- Chip On the Shoulder
- Throwing Things or Snapping Easily
- Stress

Stress is said to be the sociably acceptable term for anger, and I think we can all admit that we have experienced stress on some level. So if you thought you were escaping this topic or reading it for your spouse or father, I remind you that this journey is for YOU. In pursuit of greater intimacy and identity with the Father, we need to come to a new level of wholeness, and especially in this area of anger because it hinders communication with God and intimacy with others.

As we all have seen, anger damages relationships, and creates relational distance between parents and children. It is one of the key factors in divorce, and causes us to have hardened hearts, losing our sensitivity to those around us. It also has tremendous ramifications on our bodies. Anger weakens our immune system and increases our blood pressure. Anger causes mistrust and usually is attached closely to withholding forgiveness. Anger makes us feel powerless, and powerless people drain the lives of those around us, thus usually leaving us isolated.

I might remind you that ANGER is not a fruit of the Spirit. The Word says that people will know we are followers of Jesus by our fruit[45], so we must realize that anger can cripple not only our testimony, but can lead nonbelievers to question Christians. In anger, we provoke others to almost fear or avoid our presence, which comes against the calling to be LOVE, and as followers of Jesus we should care about the impact our lives are having for or against the Kingdom of God on earth. We need to be intentional to go deeper in our souls and remove the roots of anger, not only for ourselves, but because we owe it to those who do life with us.

We also need to realize that we have control over anger, it does not have control over us.

You may question this statement, but if you were yelling at your children or husband and a police officer or your pastor walked up, could you stop? I am sure you would say, "Yes!" Then you *can* control your anger. Anger doesn't have to control you, but rather alert you to an area that you need to invite the Holy Spirit into for healing.

TESTIMONY:

I ministered to a woman whose husband betrayed her by having an emotional affair with another woman. She went through all of the emotions that led to anger. She felt shame and inferiority. She was hurt and full of rejection. She sought to heal and save her marriage, but she found herself always erupting. She would be in line at the grocery store, and see an article of celebrities splitting because of an affair, and all of the sudden she was snappy with the cashier. She would listen to talk radio and hear of a man morally falling, and within moments she was finding some ridiculous reason to be yelling at her children in the back seat. She could hardly watch television for the number of reports of men with questionable character that would stir up a pool of rejection in her belly, and within moments someone was the target of her projection of anger.

It is quite clear looking in that she wasn't upset with the cashier, her children, or the television, but rather she had not fully dealt with the pain she had chosen to bury deep. Instead, she chose *not* to be needy or weak, which created an even greater challenge because it became a stronghold, causing her to depend on her strength rather than on God. When anything reminded her of the betrayal, she would almost instantly erupt towards what seemed to be the issue, yet she was missing it completely. However, her family wasn't missing it, and instead were becoming wounded by the wounds of their mother.

The challenge is that we live in a culture that encourages you to stuff and wear a mask, but neither ever lead to healing. This doesn't mean that you air your 'dirty laundry' to the world, but that you find safe people, and the feet of Jesus to expose your heart and grieve appropriately. It is necessary to grieve. It is necessary to expose hurts and wounds. You have permission to *feel*. It is actually healthy to feel. Our hope is that we can recognize the root of our pain, and surrender to the inner working of the Holy Spirit to relieve us from this pain. With the healing of what lies beneath, the anger will dissipate.

Another scenario that I see often when walking people through freedom ministry has to do with ones' voice. It appears that many women have felt at some time in their lives that what they had to say or what they felt didn't matter. They felt voiceless and powerless, and as they became adults, they vowed that no one would ever have the power to quench their voice again, therefore anytime they felt the slightest bit dismissed, unseen, or unvalued, they would erupt, give the cold shoulder, use sarcasm, or become snappy. Another common response is to let this hidden anger cause us to be offended by people around us, though it has *nothing* to do with them.

Here is a prime example: A woman in your small group can ask for the opinions of others regarding an upcoming event. Accidentally and innocently, she overlooks you, but in your mind you have been rejected, hurt, and have vowed to isolate yourself from this group of women that God intended to encourage you. You believe you are voiceless again, and *they* are the cause of your rejection. The truth is that they haven't made you feel voiceless, but rather your parents or a teacher made you feel voiceless as a child and your childhood anger was never dealt with, so even though you are thirty-five, you responded like a nine year old little girl that needed to be heard, and when she wasn't heard she removed herself from communion with others.

None of us are immune from anger, unfortunately. We have all felt the emotions that birth anger. Tragically, we live in a culture that teaches you to put on your big girl panties and move on, instead of taking the time to connect your heart with His, bringing every single raw emotion before the throne of Grace for Him to speak truth and love into the deepest, darkest places. He never meant for us to bury roots of hurt, rejection, and bitterness, but rather to be rooted in His love[46].

I want you to look over the symptoms of anger and see which ones you are currently seeing in your own life. Then, spend some time with the Holy Spirit recalling what triggers these symptoms.

The symptoms of anger include:
- Irritation, Agitation, and Frustration
- Sarcasm
- Cold Shoulder or Silent Treatment
- Fury or Rage
- Fleeing from conflict
- Chip On the Shoulder
- Throwing Things or Snapping Easily

- Stress

What symptoms of anger do I carry?

_____

_____

_____

What triggers these symptoms?

_____

_____

_____

Where did this root of anger come from?

_____

_____

_____

_____

_____

Ask the Holy Spirit to show you if you are angry with God. It is safe to be transparent here.

_____

_____

_____

_____

He speaks to my heart...

His intention was that we would lay our heart at His feet and allow His perfect love to take root. When we stuff our emotions, pain, and disappointments, we allow anger, shame, and fear to take root. Perhaps you should meditate on Ephesians 3 today, asking for His Perfect Love to uproot the places where anything but love has grown.

_____

_____

_____

_____

_____

_____

_____

_____

_____

_____

_____

_____

_____

_____

_____

_____

_____

_____

CHAPTER TWENTY:

FACING YOUR FEAR

There is no fear in love. But perfect love drives out fear, because fear has to do with punishment. The one who fears is not made perfect in love.
1 John 4:18

Fear is the antagonist of the call to love. It comes against the very nature of God—perfect love—that commissions us to, above all else, *love!*[47] In Paul's first Epistle to Timothy he says:

For God has not given us a spirit of fear and timidity, but of power, love, and self-discipline. [48]

This spirit of fear that is sabotaging our destiny, our relationships, our sanity, and our livelihood is not a spirit from God, but rather one that seeks to blind us from our power, our mind of Christ, and our ability to heal through love.

What is fear robbing from your life? Is it stealing your peace at night and keeping you up, fearing the days ahead? Is it damaging your relationships, making you paranoid that you can't trust people, even those you love because you fear betrayal? Is it keeping you complacent in life, robbing your dreams because you fear failure? We need to understand our core fears, because you will find that they are having more impact on your life than you realize. Especially in marriage, we can see these core fears become key sources of friction.

TESTIMONY:

When Todd and I married, we were bringing together two families and a Uhaul full of baggage. We were seeking to navigate through the dynamics of blending two families together and all that 'blending' entails, while trying to connect as newlyweds. {I might add that this may just be impossible to do peacefully!} We both loved the Lord, and were fully immersed in ministry, yet there was great conflict in our marriage. I was very discouraged, and even heart broken, to be quiet honest. I had been careful to marry a 'man of God,' so I had placed high expectations on our marriage—too high of expectations, if I'm being honest. When I met Todd, he was the most passionate preacher I had ever seen, and I was taken captive almost immediately by this beautiful being I called my SMOG {Sexy Man of God.}

Todd was so full of the Word, and I was enamored by the way God spoke to him. His knowledge of the Word was unlike anything I had witnessed. It was almost too good to be true, right? He was handsome, charming, loved Jesus, a preacher, and a doting daddy, so I was certain I had met prince charming, and my life was about to be transported to the Cinderella Castle.

I would soon learn that my expectations were far from my reality. Todd walked very strongly—not kindly— in authority in our home. I began to walk on egg shells, fearing his eruptions, and the atmosphere of our home was far from the peace I had imagined. Coupled with this fear of his anger, I didn't trust his words. He hadn't been completely honest on a few occasions, and it lead to me questioning the slightest comment he made. Ultimately, my internal battle led to chronic health issues. Feeling like I was at my end, I dug deeper into freedom ministry and realized that I had a core fear that was being triggered by our marriage—fear of being victim to fraud. In my past, I had been in a relationship with a man that turned out to be a fraud. He lied about his family, his finances, his spiritual life, and his children. When I found out that all of this was a lie and I confronted him, I became a victim of abuse.

So as it turned out, my relationship with Todd was not simply a couple with communication challenges, but rather it was tapping into my deepest core fear, causing it to not only effect our marriage, but also my health. When I shared this fear with my husband, he realized, too, that his authoritative nature came from his own core fear of being dominated by a woman. Todd had come from a marriage where he felt his previous wife was very dominant and basically ran their home. As a result of the pain from his failed marriage, he vowed to never let a woman rule his home again. In effort to relieve his own pain, he began to rule our home with an iron fist which caused tension in our home. As we were able to see that our core fears were causing our friction, we were able to respond appropriately. We had to bring our fears and past wounds to Jesus to begin the healing process rather than continue denying our pain. We became more intentional about understanding our core fears and creating a safe environment for both of us in our home. We chose to look in rather than to point out when future friction manifest in our relationship too.

If you are a blended family, I highly recommend pursing freedom ministry together. As I minster to blended couples, it is inevitable that our past failings are affecting our current marriages—no one is immune to the struggles of blending. I believe all marriages can thrive, and it is worth doing the work to live in a healthy, whole home.

Before I began my life in ministry, I spent fourteen years in pharmaceutical sales. The medical side of me loves to explore what science proves true in the Word of God. Dr. Caroline Leaf has mastered proving that science is aligned to the Word of God. After over thirty years of studying the human brain, she has shown that the brain is neuroplastic, which means it can be molded or changed. She claims that in just four days of taking your thoughts of fear captive and replacing them with faith, you can see visible changes in the brain. She says that we process everything through fear or faith, and behind every fear is a lie. She speaks about two different kinds of fears: Rational and Irrational.

Rational Fears are God given fears that keep us safe and alert to danger. These are good fears that guard us.

Irrational fear is where the enemy seeks to establish strongholds of fear in our lives. Irrational fears come from lies.

We know that Satan is the father of lies. If lies birth fear—as Dr. Leaf is convinced they do—we need to be intentional about coming out of agreement with these fears, otherwise we are partnering not with God but with Satan, giving him free rein in our thought life. No wonder we are tormented with thoughts that keep us from the mind of Christ. Fear includes worry, anxiety, rage, impatience, and irritation, and all of these produce toxic attitudes and toxic responses.

It is important we recognize ways that fear can enter our lives, especially as parents, so that we can be more mindful about doors that could be open in our homes. Fear can enter from watching horror movies or occult practices. Trauma can obviously open doors to fear of abuse, fear of not being safe, or fear of man. Neglect can open doors to fear of abandonment, rejection and poverty. Even religious bondage can open doors to fear of not measuring up or losing salvation. Many denominations, as we have discussed, create fear around the gift of the Holy Spirit. We also inherit fears from our family such as fear of tragedy, fear of disease or death, fear of poverty, fear of failure, or fear of storms.

Three of the most prevalent fears are fear of rejection, fear of death, and fear of failure. Our deepest need is for the love of God, so it makes sense that rejection is one of the greatest fears. It is also interesting that our deepest need is also the solution to overcome fear: LOVE! The Word of God says: *Perfect love cast out fear.* God, in His infinite wisdom, knew the strategy of the enemy and equipped us to overcome everything Satan brings to the table. I love how Psalm 23:5 speaks:

*You prepare a table before me in the presence of
my enemies. You anoint my head with oil;
my cup overflows.*

When the enemy comes, our God begins setting the banquet of our life before us so that we might feast. So the next time fear seeks to creep into your life, I want you to just close your eyes and imagine that feast. *Focus on the feast!* The more we keep our eyes on His truth and our focus on His power, the less likely fear can attach to us. It must flee!

The answer to releasing fear is RECOG-NIZING what doors we have opened, and where fear is growing, and inviting Perfect Love—that cast out fear— into those areas where fear is rooted.

Submit to God, resist the devil and he will flee.
James 4:7

Father, please show me the places in my life where I have opened the door to fear.

_____

_____

_____

_____

What event happened that introduced this fear?

_____

_____

_____

_____

What lie was introduced into my life as a result of fear?

_____

_____

_____

What is your truth about this lie?

_____

_____

_____

Dismantle This Lie:
Recognize the Lie.
Repent for the Lie.
Renounce the Lie.
Receive His truth.
Replace the Lie with His truth.

He speaks to my heart...

Dear Heavenly Father,
I recognize that I have acted in Fear instead of faith. I
come out of agreement with fear, and I rest in your
perfect love. Father, speak to me now.....

_____

_____

_____

_____

_____

_____

_____

_____

_____

_____

_____

_____

_____

_____

_____

_____

_____

_____

What Next?

My experience is that this is a journey to freedom and healing. The enemy will come to steal the work that has been done here, but you have grown in wisdom through this process. You now see with clarity who your enemy truly is, how he operates, and you have a strategy to dismantle him.

You should use this journal when you see patterns that are entangling you, assignments that seem to be following you, and pain that just doesn't seem to release you. You can always come back and walk through this journey again and again. I have found that some things are only brought to the surface when we are capable of dealing with them. There were some lies in my life that if I had found earlier, they could have sent me deeper into a pit, but God's timing is always perfect. As we go deeper in the well of our souls, what has laid dormant longest seems to rise to the top. Just when we think we have come to a new place of freedom, the deepest darkest places of our hearts are exposed, because it is only then that we are prepared to face them with grace rather than shame or unworthiness.

So you may wonder what this process has to do with Esther? I am so glad you asked. I believe the Father revealed to me that in her 'soaking' season, she too was tending to the condition of her heart. If we are fragmented, broken, or bound to lies, we can never fully step into the intimacy, identity, and destiny God has for us. When we are whole, it is less about us and more about Him. When we are whole, our voices speak from a new level of authority. When we are whole, we can stand against the enemy and regain territory for the Kingdom of God on this earth. I believe the Father is looking for women to release divine revelation, authority, and strategies that will heal our land and birth the next great awakening. As long as we are deceived by the enemy, we are too wounded to carry out such an assignment. We can learn from mountain climbers that wounds don't heal at high levels. To go higher with Him, we must be willing to go deeper within.

I pray that this season of 'soaking' has removed barriers to intimacy with the Father, and opened new channels to hear and experience Him. Assignments are given in the Secret Place —the place you meet alone with God—so seek His heart and your assignments will come organically.

My intent is to follow this book with:

- An E-Course titled "Love Your Life: Live Free"

- *Freedom in Marriage* video series with Todd Foster

- *Spiritual Practices That Draw You Into The Secret Place*

- *Unlocking Divine Assignments: Understanding the Courts of Heaven*

You can find Rochelle @ www. rochellefoster.com.

NOTES

Over the years, I have gleaned from a number of men and women who are pioneers in the area of freedom ministry including the freedom team at Gateway Church in Dallas, Texas, Elijah House Prayer Ministry, Golden Monarch Inner Healing Center in Abilene, Texas, and Sozo Prayer Ministry at Bethel Church in Redding, California. One thing consistent in every ministry is the desire to connect people intimately to the Father. All methods support the need to seek answers from the true source, God, through Jesus and the Holy Spirit.

In addition to these ministries, I have personally walked numerous women through freedom and prayer ministry sessions where I have witnessed decades of bondage broken off of women through encounters with Jesus. This book takes pieces of my gleaning, and pieces of my experience in my own pursuit of freedom, along with revelation from the Holy Spirit, and hopes to awaken you to a life that you love!

SCRIPTURAL REFERENCES BY NOTES:

1. Colossians 1:20
2. Deuteronomy 31:6
3. Genesis 35:1-15
4. Joshua 4
5. 1 Kings 19:21
6. Genesis 4:1
7. 2 Corinthians 12:10
8. Romans 2:4
9. 2 Corinthians 4:4
10. Ephesians 4:18
11. 1 Corinthians 12:9
12. Ephesians 3:19
13. Psalm 139:16

14. Psalm 37:4
15. John 19:30
16. Ephesians 2:18
17. 1 Peter 5:8
18. 2 Corinthians 11:14
19. Luke 11
20. Psalm 51:6
21. Hosea 4:6
22. Matthew 16:25
23. Acts 20:35
24. Matthew 7:14
25. Hebrews 6:19
26. Exodus 20:3, Deuteronomy 5:7
27. Matthew 16:24
28. Ephesians 4:15
29. Psalm 46:10
30. John 17:3
31. 1 Samuel 16:7
32. Luke 22:42
33. John 10:10
34. Matthew 18: 21-35
35. Psalm 34:18
36. John 1:12
37. Ecclesiastes 3:11
38. Ezekiel 36:25
39. James 4:7
40. Psalm 7:11, Luke 18
41. Ephesians 6
42. Luke 6:45
43. Romans 2:4
44. Luke 6:45
45. Matthew 7:16
46. Ephesians 3
47. 1 Peter 4:8
48. 2 Timothy 1:7

The Author

Rochelle and her husband, Todd, pastor The Well , a church in McComb, Mississippi. The Well is a multi-cultural, multi-denominational church that has a vision to impact the culture of cities across our nation for the Kingdom of God by being a source of revival. The Fosters have made Freedom Ministry a vital part of their church culture, believing that it takes free people to free people. As believers, they feel we should all pursue freedom in effort to advance the Kingdom of God on Earth.

Rochelle is passionate about teaching freedom ministry through Women's Conferences, and her website rochellefoster.com. She is the author of the "Sweeteas" children's series, and "He Gave Me Pearls." She is the proud mother of her beautifully blended family: Joy, Jadyn, Holland Rose, Houston, and Jackson. The Fosters reside in McComb, Mississippi.

SPECIAL THANKS

Thank you to my dear friend, Heidi, who invested countless hours helping me sift through all that was in my head and heart to get this into your hands. I am forever grateful!

Thank you to the women of The Well who inspire me daily by their beautiful lives that speak to the power of God to free us. You are refreshment to my soul! Thank you to the many women that have shared their stories of freedom with me encouraging me to press on when– at times– I could have given up! Thank you to the beautiful faces of St. Simons Island, Georgia, and Joplin, Missouri, that I will forever be knit together with.

Thank you to my SMOG, Todd, who has loved me through my mess and been my greatest champion. Thank you to my parents and babies for embracing a less than perfect daughter and mom and making my life full!

Thank you to Darlene Grieme, my agent, who has supported me–and the lioness inside of me–even when my boldness caused many doors to shut! Thank you for letting me be me!

CPSIA information can be obtained
at www.ICGtesting.com
Printed in the USA
FFOW03n1449300118
44733589-44765FF